God Is at Eye Level

God Is at Eye Level

Photography as a Healing Art

by Jan Phillips

Award-winning photographer and author of
Marry Your Muse

A publication supported by
THE KERN FOUNDATION

Quest Books
Theosophical Publishing House
Wheaton, Illinois ♦ Chennai (Madras), India

    The Theosophical Publishing House
    P.O. Box 270
    Wheaton, IL 60189-0270

A publication of the Theosophical Publishing House,
a department of the Theosophical Society in America

Cover and text design and typesetting by Beth Hansen-Winter

Library of Congress Cataloging-in-Publication Data

Phillips, Jan.
God is at eye level: photography as a healing art / Jan Phillips.
      p.   cm.
Includes bibliographical references.
ISBN 0-8356-0785-2
1. Photography in psychotherapy.   2. Photography—Therapeutic use.
I. Title.
RC489.P56 P47 2000
615.8'515—dc21   99-045606

5 4 3 2 1 ★ 00 01 02 03 04 05 06 07

Printed in Hong Kong through
Global Interprint, Santa Rosa, California

Dedication

This book is dedicated to all the photographers who are using their vision in the service of community and compassion, making images that inspire us and remind us of the beauty that is ours to safeguard and honor.

Contents

Acknowledgments

I give thanks, first of all, to God, Light Itself, whose radiance continually draws me in and draws me out.

To Annie O'Flaherty and my family for creating the circle that holds me up and allows me the privilege of doing this work.

To Cathy Conheim and Donna Brooks, for your unremitting support and generosity.

To Hannelore Hahn, visionary and founder of the International Women's Writing Guild, which has been the springboard for so many of us into the life of our dreams.

To all the women across the U.S. and Canada who have invited me into your communities to share my workshops and be fueled by your imaginations.

To Brenda Rosen, editor extraordinaire, for your vision and exquisite sense of the spirit of things; and to Beth Hansen-Winter for your eye and hand in the design of this book.

To the San Diego Musettes for your wisdom, humor, and joyful presence in my life.

To the Foundation for Women for weaving such a vast and vital circle of support.

To the Syracuse Cultural Workers for creating and sharing images that ignite awareness and inspire action on behalf of the planet and all its creatures.

To Andrew Harvey and Alex Grey for the profound difference your words and your work have made in my life.

And to all the persons around the world whose faces I have photographed, cherished, learned from, and shared, to you I bow gratefully and lovingly.

Introduction

*There are two ways of spreading light: to be
the candle or the mirror that reflects it.*

EDITH WHARTON

One fall day, while I was splitting maple logs into firewood on my farm in upstate New York, a neighbor pulled up in his '57 pickup, rolled down his dusty window, and shouted above the rumbling engine, "You know, that wood's going to heat you three times."

"Oh, yeah?" I replied, wondering what he was talking about.

"Yup," he said. "The first time is now, when you're working up a sweat splitting it into firewood. The second time is when you're sitting in front of the fire, toasty warm as it crackles away. And the third time is when you haul out the ashes. Can't ask much more than that from a tree," he laughed, as he roared off down the road.

That neighbor loved wood—loved to work with it, walk through forests full of it, talk about it. His observations were as deep as the passion he held. When spring came, and I was wandering through the forest hunting for images with my 35mm, I thought of that neighbor. I thought about his passion for the woods, how it nurtured him, brought him to life. And I thought about my passion for photography, how it comforts me, brings me to life. Photography, I thought, heals three times.

The first time is when I am in search of the image, present only to *that which is,* focused on the moment at hand. By virtue of this absorption in the now, I am released from the often painful grip of past and future. The second healing belongs to the person being photographed, the honored recipient of pure attention, healed by an artist's loving gaze. The third healing occurs when we view a photograph as an outside observer and are moved by its power or beauty. The chance to see the world through another's lens, to be transported to another time, another place, another reality, can heal and transform our own.

This book is the story of photography's renewing magic, of times and places where healing has happened while photographs were taken or seen. For twenty-five years I have been scanning the world outside me for images that mirror the world within. I study eyes for a spark that's familiar, gaze at mountains until I feel my strength, delight in thresholds I stumble across, reminded of openings I have yet to explore. Every step in the process of taking pictures is a step toward the light, an experience of the holy, an encounter with the God who is at eye level, whose image I see wherever I look.

This was one of my favorite pictures when I was little. I adored my big sister and felt so safe holding her hand. And that plaid coat. I loved that, too, because my mom had made it for me from one of my favorite aunt's skirts. When I had moments of doubt that I was lovable, I'd pull this picture out and just sit with it for awhile.

Even now, when I pull out some of these images, stories the size of myths come to mind. Stacks of old snapshots are like treasure chests, overflowing with valuable gems, clues to the deeper mystery of who we are.

CHAPTER 1

Through the Eyes of a Child

There is always one moment in childhood when the door opens and lets the future in.

GRAHAM GREENE

As a child, I was always fascinated by photographs. Whenever I was lonely or out-of-sorts, I'd pull my mother's shoebox full of snapshots off the shelf and go through each one, peering into the lives of people I knew and people I didn't.

The photographs had a soothing power, and I returned to them time and again as one might visit a chapel or an old friend or a favorite mountain stream. They transported me to another world, an inner world of calm and the certain comfort that I was a member of a tribe, a face among other faces, one among the many. They helped me *re*member myself and reconnect to the larger family.

My mom had grown up on a farm, one of fourteen kids. Those small black-and-white photographs of her childhood said more to me than words ever could about family togetherness and the joys of working and playing. When I'd hold in my little hands a picture of my mother's family in the steam-filled sugar shanty, tasting the first batch of

What did you do as a child that created timelessness, that made you forget time? There lies the myth to live by.

JOSEPH CAMPBELL

My enjoyment of life began with my eyes.

RUTH BERNHARD

maple syrup, or bundled up for a winter ride in the horse-drawn sleigh, or square dancing in the barn's huge hayloft with dozens of neighbors joining in, I'd smile, knowing that I was a member of a family who knew how to transform ordinary events into adventures.

When I'd come upon my grandfather's picture in his sailor's uniform and read the newspaper clipping that told about how he'd enlisted in support of his sons who'd been drafted, I'd swell with childish pride. My grandfather was a hero to me, and so I belonged to hero stock. And in the photos of the airport he built after the war to teach people how to fly or of his farm-machinery store that became a family business, I glimpsed my own future. That grown-up life of freedom and independence and fun was waiting for me, too. This was my family. I belonged to them, and they belonged to me. With those four-inch snapshots in my hands, I was safe, in good company, the luckiest kid I knew.

There were pictures of me in that box as well—me sitting next to my favorite baby-sitter, Joanie Murphy, who had her arm draped protectively around my shoulders, or crowded together with the neighborhood kids, or in my favorite dress, the one with the puffy sleeves that I hated but with my initials embroidered over my heart. My mom had embroidered those initials. She had been so proud of me at my kindergarten graduation when I sang "Let the Sunshine In" louder than anyone else—and the photo of me in my cap and gown held all that joy for me. Some days I'd go searching in the shoebox for that picture, just so I could have that memory and feel the warm glow of my mother's love and pride again.

Each photo in that shoebox was a kind of mirror. With the eyes of a child, I entered through them into the world of the image. Each snapshot was a story, calling on my imagination to fill it out, find my place in it, take my lesson from it. Collectively, metaphorically, they conjured up a mighty tree of which I was a small but important branch. They rooted me, nourished me. They drew my gaze upward towards a future I knew I could grow up to inhabit.

Looking back, I realize it was not only the power of the images themselves, but the very act of focusing, of being totally attentive, that comforted me. When I look through my lens now, focused only on what is before me, I am grounded and healed in that same wonderful way. My vision is clear, and I am one with whatever I am looking at, as I was one with those images forty years ago. Not alone, not apart from, not afraid. Full of joy, as we all can be, when we look with the eyes of a child, in rapt attention.

Reflections

1. Try to remember the activities you turned to as a child when you felt lonely and out-of-sorts. Do you do any of these things now? How have you replaced them?

2. Make or find a photograph of something that calms you when you see it. Frame the photo and put it wherever you spend the most time in your day.

3. If you have a video camera, videotape a selection of your best old and new family photographs. Put your video to music and show it at your next family gathering.

In the act of deeply seeing, we transcend the boundaries between the self and the otherness of the world, momentarily merging with the thing seen.

ALEX GREY

Many people I know have a love affair with photography. They're filled with stories of transformations that occurred as they discovered photography's power to soothe and mend the broken wing.

I did not come to photography looking for magic. I came looking for a way to speak my pain. In the process of finding images to portray my darkness, I passed through the shadows into the light. Now I am one of photography's many lovers, devoted to the art of seeing and revealing.

Every second I spend looking through a lens waiting for someone's beauty to surface, a cloud to move, the light to turn from gray to gold; every hour that passes as I stand in the darkroom with safelight shining, transforming the negative into a positive, I am warmed and transformed.

There's something holy about this work, something healing about this search for the light. Like the pilgrim's journey, it's heaven all the way.

CHAPTER 2

Seeing Our Way Clear

The creative process, so far as we are able to follow it at all, consists in the unconscious activation of an archetypal image, and in elaborating and shaping this image into the finished work. By giving it shape, the artist translates it into the language of the present, and so makes it possible for us to find our way back to the deepest springs of life.

CARL JUNG

In 1967, when I was eighteen, I entered a convent. After two years, I was dismissed for "lack of a religious disposition." The news that I had to leave came suddenly; one night, without warning, my parents appeared to take me home. I was given no chance to say good-bye to the friends I would be leaving behind. As I was ushered through the basement corridors, my novice director said sternly, "You are not allowed to communicate with the sisters. They will keep you in their prayers."

Nine months later, as the birthday of my best friend in the novitiate was approaching, I decided to make her a birthday present. I would create an album of photographs and quotations that might convey, in the language of images, all that I wished I could say to her. Since mail was censored by the order's superiors, I tried to keep the album as impersonal as

> *I have always taken pictures the way people keep journals and diaries. It's a way of ordering my reactions to the world, of placing my ideas and feelings in a concrete form outside myself, of breaking my isolation.*
>
> DIANA MICHENER

possible. No card. No letter. No notes on the page other than quotations from authors we'd loved, songs we'd sung together, prayers and poems we'd passed back and forth. The photographs had to do most of the work. In their silent language, they had to reveal me, speak the words I couldn't say, carry the weight of my tangled feelings, my attempts to get past the pain.

With a Kodak Instamatic in hand, I went out day after day in search of pictures to portray my struggle to reassemble my life, to regain my footing, and rekindle my joy. I rummaged for images that would *be* the words I wanted to speak, that could whisper my voice in every color and shade of gray.

I went to the mountains and the desert, the ocean and the forests. I found myself reflected in parched desert floors, redwood saplings, homeless park dwellers. I photographed footsteps dissolving in the tide, my body against a twelve-foot cross, my shadow on the steps leading to a locked church door. Images of crashing waves and toppled sand castles, friends huddled on a moonlit beach, a woman alone strumming a guitar, birds

We do not make photographs with our cameras. We make them with our minds, with our hearts, with our ideas.

ARNOLD NEWMAN

soaring into golden sunsets—each reflected something I felt but could not say, a metaphor for a sentiment I could not share.

As the photos were developed, I studied each one, looking for the emotions they contained—finding strength in one, fear in another, loneliness and joy and conviction in others. Everything I had experienced since I left the Motherhouse was captured in those prints—the rejection that seemed to have come from God, the loss of my community, the loneliness for my friends, the fear of what was to come, the doubt about my own worth, the disappointment that I could not have the life I felt called to, the anger at being dismissed without a chance to defend myself.

In my quest for photographs that would tell my story, I revealed myself to myself in a new way. Photography pushed me to understand each feeling in order to portray it. Every detail mattered immensely. The light mattered; the shadows mattered; the mood and tone and contrast mattered. There was nothing else on the page—only one image after another, saying:

Dear Lois,

Here I am. Here is how I'm doing. This is what I'm thinking. This page is my loss. And here is the joy I am trying to hold onto. Here is the fragment of my faith that remains. Here is my long, lonely howl in the night.

Making that album was a healing ritual from beginning to end. It gave me a new way to let grief out—to see it,

My photographs are never straight reportage, never merely objective. In them all, I have expressed myself, nothing else.

ANDRÉ KERTÉSZ

A photograph is not only an image, an interpretation of the real; it is also a trace, something directly stenciled off the real, like a footprint or a death mask.

SUSAN SONTAG

In every human being, there are capacities for creative action. . . . This need of human beings is almost as deep-seated as their need for air to breathe and food to eat.

BERENICE ABBOTT

experience it, understand it. In the process, my sorrow became less a malignancy I was bent on destroying and more a companion I was seeking to befriend. As I glued each photograph onto the page, I was touched by its power, its ability to give voice to my silence, to shed light on my darkness.

It almost didn't matter, by the time it was done, if the book made it to Lois after all. It had done far more work than I'd ever imagined, helping me to accept my sorrow and express it in the truest way I could.

As it turned out, when the book arrived, Lois was summoned by the novice director, who told her to read it right there in her office. Page by page, Lois studied the photos, read the quotations, and entered the world between my lines. She knew then that I was struggling, trying to hold on, and that I was a very long way from home. But she kept that knowing to herself and so was permitted to take the book back to her room.

Carl Jung wrote that in the process of giving shape to archetypal images, we find our way back to our deepest, truest selves. In the course of manifesting what we hold within, of transforming spirit and ideas into matter and language, we experience the holy delight of creation. And as we give form to spirit, so are we informed by it and healed by it. As we express the Divine through art, so do we experience the Divine within.

Photography, I discovered, is as much about seeing inside ourselves as it is about looking out at the world. All creative activity joins spirit to matter and so can transform. But photography is special. It is all about focus and attention, image and shadow, figure and ground, darkness and light.

A great photograph is a full expression of what one feels.

ANSEL ADAMS

It doesn't matter if you don't have a sophisticated camera, if you have never studied photography, if the photographs you take are far from professional. What matters is that something intimate and precious and sacred is being brought to life and shared with another. That's what healing is all about.

Reflections

Everything in life that we really accept undergoes a change.

KATHERINE MANSFIELD

1. Imagine that you have one roll of film with which to convey your response to an event in your life. Choose an event that carries some emotional weight. Be present to all the emotions it conjures up and decide which emotions you'd most like to release or transform. How would you represent these emotions in your images? What time of day would be most suitable? What colors come to mind? What objects? What forces of nature? What elements? Now, if you wish, take your camera, and shoot the roll of film.

2. Many people have favorite quotations that inspire and help them keep faith during dark times. Select one of your favorites, and illustrate it photographically. When you review your photos, pick the one that works best, enlarge it, and create a poster with your image and the quotation.

3. Find a friend who is willing to be photographed, and choose an emotion you want to explore photographically. It might be something like mystery, or freedom, or playfulness. Decide on locations, backgrounds, colors, textures, compositions that represent this concept, and spend a few hours and rolls of film together addressing the theme. You and your friend might even take turns photographing each other.

Every creative person has a second date of birth, and one which is more important than the first: that on which he discovers what his true vocation is.

BRASSAÏ

I started shooting before I had the slightest clue about lighting, composition, tone, texture. It was all about content, at first—the simple gathering of evidence that I had been somewhere. "Here is a picture of my motorcycle. Here are the Blue Ridge Mountains in the background. See where I have been." It took a long time to understand that photographs could record a lot more than my itinerary. They could say who I was, what I loved about life, and what I found along the way.

CHAPTER 3

Shifting the Focus

The greatest thing a human soul ever does in this world is to see something and tell what it saw in a plain way. Hundreds of people can talk for one who can think, and thousands can think for one who can see. To see clearly is poetry, philosophy, and religion, all in one.

JOHN RUSKIN

When I told my photographer friend Bill Gandino that I was about to ride my Honda 400 from Syracuse to Southern California, he shrieked, "You can't go across country on a motorcycle without a camera!"

"I *have* a camera," I responded proudly, pulling my old Instamatic out of my peacoat pocket. "Not a 110!" he yelped. "What, are you nuts? Come on, we're going shopping for a *real* camera."

He was a regular at the camera store and a good haggler, so I ended up with a used Pentax Spotmatic for $100. Totally manual. No automatic anything. It seemed pretty clunky to me, compared to my slender 110, but Gandino assured me it was just what I needed. "Come on. Let's go to Pizza Hut. I'll teach you how to use it."

On the back of his placemat, he drew a picture of my camera from the side, with a detailed view of the aperture and shutter. Then he explained that the aperture works like

To take photographs means to recognize—simultaneously and within a fraction of a second—both the fact itself and the rigorous organization of visually perceived forms that give it meaning. It is putting one's head, one's eye, and one's heart on the same axis. It is a way of shouting, of freeing oneself, not of proving or asserting one's own originality. It is a way of life.

HENRI CARTIER-BRESSON

the iris of the human eye, opening wider when it's dark to let in more light, closing down when the light is bright. That part was easy, but the shutter concept was a little trickier. It was hard to draw, so he tried to explain in words. "The shutter is like a curtain letting light into a room. When you open it, light floods in, and when you close it, the room stays dark. That's what happens inside the camera when you release the shutter. It lets in light to expose the film." I got that part, but when he tried to explain the connection between the aperture and the shutter, I was lost.

Over pepperoni pizza, Bill drilled me and drilled me. Open up the aperture to blur the background. Close down if you want everything in focus. Use a fast shutter speed to stop the motion. Don't shoot under 1/60 of a second without a tripod. Take a light reading off the palm of your hand if your subject is back-lit. Shoot with Kodachrome 64 for the best results. Take slides if you want to publish. By the time lunch was over, my head was spinning.

A few days later I strapped my backpack onto my motorcycle and headed west. It was the end of September, and I nearly froze by the time I hit Pittsburgh. So I veered left and headed for Florida, arriving the same day as Hurricane Agnes.

Trying to tent on the beaches with gale winds blowing was an adventure, and I did my best to capture it on film. I shot my way through the cotton fields of Mississippi, the French Quarter of New Orleans, the barren foreverness of Texas, the white sand desert of New Mexico, and around the rim of the Grand Canyon. By the time I reached the Pacific twenty-eight days later, I had eight rolls of slides to develop.

Those who do original work in any field do so because they mine themselves deeply and bring up what is personal.

RALPH STEINER

If the photographer is not a discoverer, he is not an artist.

PAUL STRAND

When I picked them up, I was dismayed to discover I could make out only a few of the photos. The rest were a blur of shadows and white lights, fuzzy fingertips, double exposures, and a bunch of other maladies I couldn't diagnose.

That week, I signed up for an adult education photography class at the local high school, determined to get this 35mm thing down. We learned about film speed, aperture

control, shutter speed, wide angle and telephoto lenses, and how to process film and make prints. Every week when my classmates brought in their roll of film to develop, I'd come in with two or three. The instructor would look at my contacts and say things like "interesting," "hmmm. . . ," or "you got a good one here." I could never figure out what made him think one image was better than another.

There was a lot we didn't cover. No talk of lighting or contrast or shades of gray. No

mention of lines or perspective, dramatic effects or best times to shoot. Those were up to us to find out, by trial and error.

I subscribed to every photography magazine on the market and went to every photo exhibition in town. Everywhere I went, my camera was slung around my neck, my pockets loaded with film. I spent all my money on film and photo paper, making 8" x 10" glossies of my friends and their kids and their kids' friends and their dogs. I was obsessed.

What happened as a result was that I started to get better. I began to be able to see for myself what made one photo better than another. I noticed the subtle distinctions between a snapshot and a photograph, started to wait longer behind the camera before I shot for the light to shift, an expression to change. I became as aware of the background as I was of the subject, as conscious of the emptiness as the fullness.

That was the beginning of my *seeing*—that shift in noticing not just what was in front of me, but what was behind that, and behind that. Seeing wasn't just visual anymore; it was visceral. I wasn't looking; I was searching, feeling, finding, reflecting, taking in, releasing. Once I knew what I needed to know technically, I walked unafraid into the deeper realm of vision, into that place where one looks for a match to what one feels inside.

Photography was no longer a hobby. It was a passion, an art form, a way of revealing myself to the world, a way of putting on paper what was inside of me that longed to be expressed. Bill Gandino had no idea what he started that day at Pizza Hut, when he opened those doors to a magical world. I had found my medium, and through that medium, I would come eventually to find myself.

Knowledge of what you love somehow comes to you; you don't have to read nor analyze nor study. If you love a thing enough, knowledge of it seeps into you, with particulars more real than any chart can furnish.

JESSAMYN WEST

The ultimate experience of anything is a realization of what's behind it.

MINOR WHITE

Reflections

1. Study some of your favorite photographs. Try to figure out what it is about each that evokes strong feelings in you. Notice their design, texture, composition, color. Get a feeling for the power of each of these elements, and try to be conscious of them the next time you are photographing.

2. Pick a subject that has some symbolic value, such as an old oak tree, a bridge, a mountain path. Shoot it at different times of day and at different apertures, if your camera allows this. Study the images carefully for your own responses to the changes you've made in exposure, details in focus, and other differences. Notice whether an underexposed image evokes a different feeling than an overexposed image. Notice whether the image is more powerful with more or less of the scene in focus. Carry this awareness with you as you shoot.

3. Take one step toward advancing your understanding of photography. Take a class in darkroom techniques or large-format photography, if you've already been shooting in 35mm. Go to your bookstore and pick out a new book on photography, or subscribe to a professional photo magazine, like *Aperture*. Keep your eyes open for a photography exhibit, and make a date with a friend to attend it.

4. The next time you take a trip somewhere, take your camera, and document the experience. Create a slideshow or photo album of your images so you can record and share your adventure.

A photographer who wants to see, a photographer who wants to make fine images, must recognize the value of the familiar.

FREEMAN PATTERSON

Surely it's a born intensity of witness, a mysterious urgent need to watch, *that first marks out the possible artist.*

REYNOLDS PRICE

Each of us has a distinctive way of seeing the world and representing it through imagery. Even if two photographers focus on an identical subject, their pictures will be different. They will each compose according to their creative urgings—one shooting with great depth of field; another with great depth of feeling. One cropping closely, eliminating the background; the other shooting wide with every detail in focus.

The distinction is in our passion and our intention. Over time, if we shoot authentically, follow the leanings of our heart, our body of work will become a silent testimony to who we are and what we care about. Our photographs will speak with a voice of their own, uttering our essence to all who can hear.

CHAPTER 4

Looking Like No Other

In contrast to the spoken and written word, a picture can be understood anywhere in the world. It can bridge the chasm created by differences of language and alphabet. It is a means for universal communication. It is the language of One World.

ANDREAS FEININGER

Often, during a visit to a gallery or exhibition, I've overheard people say, "What's so great about that? My kid could have painted it." Or, "Look at this photo, honey. I've thrown out better ones that this." I've thought some of these things myself, looking at images by well-known photographers that seem no more eloquent than my own photographs or those of my friends.

It's true. Many of us have the technical know-how and creative eye to shoot and print photographs every bit as stunning as those in galleries and photo books. The question is, are we *doing it?* Are we creating a body of work and putting it out there for people to see? Are we taking the time and making the effort to pack up our cameras and walk through the world with the eye and the eagerness to create images? This means studying our environment and knowing when the light is right. It means having a sense of what we're looking for, being aware of our vision, both inner and outer, and being

Surfaces reveal inner states—cameras record surfaces. I must somehow be a kind of microscope by which the underlying forces of spirit are observed and extended to others.

MINOR WHITE

Chance favors the prepared mind.

ANSEL ADAMS

ready to shoot at just that moment when the two come together.

Henri Cartier-Bresson, one of the world's best-known and most respected photographers, wrote a book in 1952 called *The Decisive Moment* in which he says that the image should be perfectly and precisely realized at the moment of exposure, not shot haphazardly and cropped later on. He looked for harmony in the lines of a scene, in the balance of shapes, and in the interrelationship of form and content. The decisive moment, for Cartier-Bresson, took place in the fraction of a second when that harmony was both revealed and recorded, "a coup of almost mystical timing," according to *World Photography* photo editor Bryn Campbell. Cartier-Bresson's ability was not simply a matter of luck, but the instinct of a photo artist who, in the words of fellow photographer Ernst Haas, "just seems to melt into any situation he photographs."

We all develop and hone these instincts in our own way, adding our own consciousness to the mix of form and content. No one in the world can make the same photograph of a person as I make, for the image my camera records reflects the *relationship* between me and the person on the other side of the lens. The face of the woman I am photographing reveals her feelings about being there in my presence. We're not separate entities—just her in the world and me in the world. Something is going on between us. Either she trusts me, or she doesn't. She feels I'm honoring her, or she doesn't. She's relaxed and comfortable, or she's not.

For me, the decisive moment includes this awareness as much as it includes an attunement to harmony of line, tonal balance, and the dance between form and content. It's loaded with emotion, expectation, spiritual connectedness, intention, energy. I'm there with my camera, focusing on a face or a scene and seeing simultaneously every detail in the background. The face I see is the outward expression of everything the person is thinking, feeling, experiencing in this moment. The background may be teeming with life, changing all the while as people pass through, clouds pass over, light turns from gray to gold. Everything is animated, shifting as I move, or recompose, or change focus. My job is to wait behind the lens until all elements converge—light, expression, feeling, form, content.

In my early days of shooting, I shot quickly, reluctant to take up too much time, feeling shy about pausing behind the lens, unclear about what I was waiting for. Now I know it's that decisive moment, that whole that contains all the parts and nothing less. I was waiting for the moment when heart and mind and eye came together on the same axis.

Once, in India, I was on a train riding in a ladies' compartment with three women and two children. We had plenty of extra room. When an elderly woman and her daughter appeared in the doorway, I motioned for them to come in. The other women in the compartment seemed perturbed, pursing their lips and shaking their heads with tight little movements. The two women in the doorway were outsiders, Muslims. No one moved over to make room. Instead, they cast their eyes down and pretended not to notice the two women looking for seats.

Finally I stood up and took the older woman's hand, leading her to my place on the

bench. There was room for only one, so she sat on the floor and motioned for her daughter to take my seat. Leaning toward me in a gesture of appreciation, the two bowed their heads and joined hands, never looking at the women who'd rejected them.

Wanting to make up for the rudeness of the others, I took out my camera and motioned a question: Could I photograph them? They nodded, and I began to shoot—the mother's head on her beautiful daughter's lap, the protective arm on the shoulder, four eyes looking into me with weariness and wonder. I shot and shot, honoring them, thanking them, loving them. Our intimacy grew with every exposure.

Though I could not speak their language, kinship glimmered in their deep dark eyes. Through smiles and expressions, they offered me something of their essence, their inner light. And I gave back my own form of light, an adoring eye, a gaze wholly focused on the radiance I perceived. Whatever distance there was between us disappeared in those moments of complete attention. We were no longer separate parts; one existed where three had been before.

As a result of that connection, something shifted for the other women in the compartment as well, a subtle opening up, a moving toward. The women who had witnessed this holy encounter rearranged their bags and created more space for the mother and daughter. They opened up their lunch baskets and passed out *dosas* and fruit, handing portions to me and to the Muslim women as well.

After our snack, I left the compartment and walked down the aisle to the train's open door, stretching out as far as I could into the hot, humid, monsoon air. In a few minutes, the woman and her daughter appeared behind me and sat down on a bale of hay across from the door. They looked up at me smiling, and I smiled right back, sitting down on the

The fundamental delusion of humanity is to suppose that I am here and you are out there.

YASUTANI ROSHI

floor and taking the mother's hand in mine. She leaned down and touched my face, stroking it in the most loving way. The daughter reached out for my other hand. As the train rolled on down the dusty track, we lingered there on the bale of hay, holding hands, rubbing palms.

The next stop was theirs. The women tugged on my arm, begging me to come with them to their home. I was sorry I couldn't, but I had to be in Delhi the next day. As the train pulled away, I hung out the door waving until they were two tiny figures in the golden light.

Shortly after I returned to my seat, a porter arrived with a bottle of Campo Cola and a huge fresh orange. Gifts, he said, from a mother and her daughter.

The photos I took that day are no better technically than anyone could have taken with a snapshooting camera. Someone could see them on a gallery wall and easily say, "What's the big deal? I could have made that photograph." But these photographs could not have existed without me. What showed up in those faces was there because of who I am, because of how I revered the women and how they perceived and responded to that reverence.

I do not need anyone to tell me that the photos I took are great. When I look at the images from that train ride, my whole day changes, my consciousness shifts, joy rises up, and I feel again my oneness with life. On my wall

I am one of those who believe that to communicate is the hope and the purpose and the impulse and the result and the test and value of all that is written and done at all, and if that little spark does not come, and with a little sheltering flash back and forth, then it's the same as being left confined within ourselves just when we wished most to reach out and touch the surrounding life that seemed so wonderful in some ways.

EUDORA WELTY

is an 11x14 print of the mother at her daughter's knee. I hung it up there so I don't forget what I want to remember—how we're connected to each other, how what we do matters, how healing can occur when we really look.

Each of us has the privilege of creating works of art that could not exist without us. We can take a subject and probe it deeply or skim the surface of many things. Our vision stems from the passion of our unique way of being and interacting in the world. All we have to do is let it go, give it voice, have it be the source of all our seeing.

Reflections

1. Take a ride on a bus, a subway, a ferry, or other form of public transportation. Hang your camera around your neck, and look for images that draw your attention. Notice how people look at you and how you look back. Ask permission to take some people shots, and observe what happens in the process. If you have fear, try to get past it. Remember, photography is about *relationship*. Work on the answer to the question, should someone ask you, "Why do you want to take my photograph?"

2. List three things or activities you feel passionate about. Choose one and develop a photo essay on some aspect of it. Look for what might be missed by someone else, and photograph that. Look for the uncommon; shoot uncommonly. If your passion is hiking, for instance, create a picture story about one hiking trail in your favorite park. Go deeply into it. Tell everything you can about that trail in images that others might not see. Expand your way of seeing. Look from the bottom up. Look through things. Look from the bird's point of view or the worm's.

If all your life means to you is water running over rocks, then photograph it, but I want to create something that would not have existed without me.

MINOR WHITE

Actually it's quite true that he's not waiting for anyone since he's not made any appointment, but the very fact that he's adopting this ultra-receptive posture means that by this he wants to help chance along, how should I say, to put himself in a state of grace with chance, so that something might happen, so that some one might drop in.

ANDRÉ BRETON

Making a portrait of someone is an honor and a privilege. It is an opportunity to look deeply into another, to see the essence of spirit as it sweeps across the surface. To do this the photographer must cross a certain threshold, enter into the presence of another being with full attention. The encounter is a holy moment, a time of communion, a chance to reflect and reveal another dimension of the Divine.

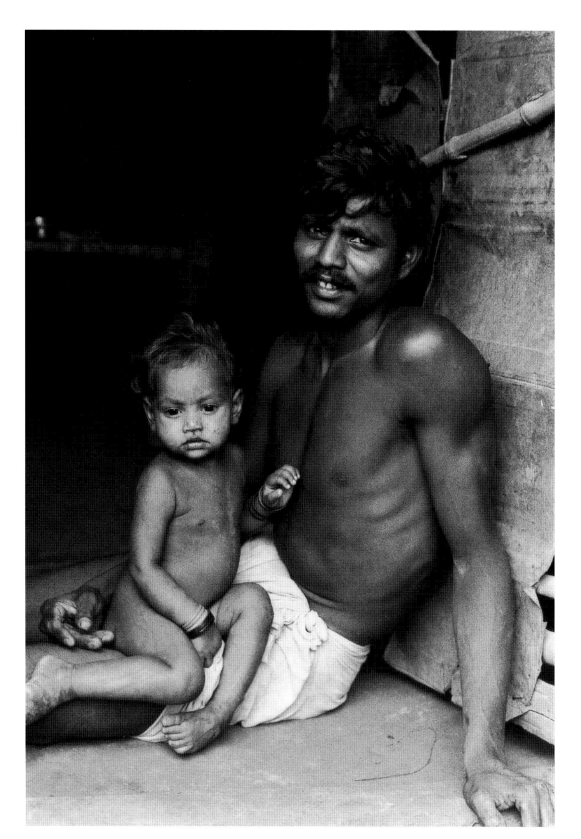

CHAPTER 5

Portrait of a Soul

When I have had such men before my camera, my whole soul has endeavored to do its duty toward them in recording faithfully the greatness of the inner as well as the outer man. The photograph thus taken has been almost the embodiment of a prayer.

JULIA MARGARET CAMERON

Often, when I'm introduced to someone as a photographer, the first question I'm asked is, "What do you shoot?" In my early years of photographing, I would respond quickly, "Everything." And that was true, for I was so caught up in the joy of shooting that everything I encountered was fair game. Every beautiful thing that caught my eye I tried to capture on film—leaves rustling on trees, rivers racing through canyons, children lost in make-believe worlds, elders huddled on park benches, moons rising, suns setting in evening skies. I went after every heart-rending, awesome image I could, storing up evidence of life's magnificence for my moments of forgetfulness and doubt.

Years later, while sorting through and editing my body of work, I discovered that I had far more portraits than anything else—a huge collection of intimate images, faces of people from all corners of the world who had sat before me and offered me the chance to

In all my photographic work, my aim was to achieve the honesty of the form, to be true to the thing itself. My satisfaction came not from taking effective photographs, but rather from the wonder of being able to capture moments that mattered to me. I tried to describe the world around me as directly as possible, to respond to its shifting truths.

DOROTHY NORMAN

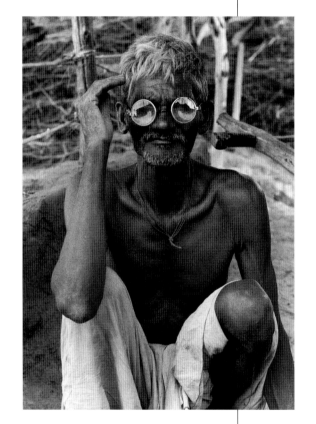

see who they were. Each portrait had its own life, carried with it the memories of what came before that moment when we were two beings caught in the singular intimacy of a photographic encounter.

Regardless of whether we spoke the same language, some form of communication was occurring, some body language was speaking our inner voices, connecting one person's questions with the other's responses. We conversed through the language of eyes and smiles—not for the sake of a Kodachrome slide, but for the joy it brings to connect with another. For me, the relationship always came first—the desire to forge a common bond with the person before me. My portraits grew out of this closeness and expressed the intimacy from which they emerged.

One day in Beijing, I encountered a man who helped me understand the importance of "relationship" to my photography. It was a bitter day in December. The Siberian winds chilled my bones on my bicycle ride from public housing, where I was staying, to the Friendship Hotel, which I often visited in search of warmth and comfort and English-speaking people.

I walked into the lobby, pretending that I lived there, wrapped in a red woolen scarf, thick hand-made mittens, and a serious Siberian fur hat. After I'd plopped into a comfortable chair, opened my camera bag, and started to load a roll of film into my Pentax, a British tourist sitting next to me started talking about photography. A photo enthusiast himself, he pulled out of his bag a fancy new gadget he was proud to show off. It was a lens with a mirror inside that allowed him to shoot at a ninety-degree angle.

"Look at this," he said proudly. "I can point my camera straight ahead and get a secret shot of someone at my side." I looked through the lens and, sure enough, a woman off to my side showed up big as life in the viewfinder.

"What do you use it for?" I asked, somewhat put off by the whole concept.

"With this, no one knows I'm taking their picture. I don't have to ask any questions. Don't have to bother with the language. It's painless, and I get some great candids."

"Oh," I said flatly. "Different strokes. I kind of like the human contact." I went back to cleaning out my camera bag, thinking sadly about what he was missing.

I *wanted* people to know I was there. I wanted to interact with them, and I wanted my images to reflect some connection, no matter how brief or limited. That connection was the healing part, the place where I learned time and again that it is not language or custom or creed that unites us, but the spirit within that's common to us all. The *greatness of the inner* person that Julia Cameron writes of recording with her camera cannot be caught with tricks and mirrors. It is something to be mined for, unearthed through our searching for what lies below.

Several years after my trip to China, I was climbing up a trail in Arizona's beautiful Canyon de Chelly. I met a Navajo man on the path and stopped to talk with him. We sat

The present challenge to the photographer is to express inner significance through outward form.

BEAUMONT NEWHALL

From the first moment I handled my lens with a tender ardor, and it has become to be as a living thing, with voice and memory and creative vigor. . . . I longed to arrest all beauty that came before me, and at length the longing has been satisfied.

JULIA MARGARET CAMERON

down on a boulder to catch our breath, and I asked him what he was going to do with the flowers in his hand.

"I'm collecting flowers to give to the goats of a woman in my clan," he said. "I love this canyon. It is good to be close to the Earth." We chewed on pieces of straw, talking back and forth about who we were and what we loved. His name was Sam Reed, and he was seventy-three years old.

Sam told me that his father had died when he was a baby, and his mother, a sheep herder and weaver, had raised Sam and his six brothers and sisters. "We went to the Friends Indian School, but we never learned about my people," he said. "I was drafted into the Marines in World War II, but war is bad business. If we want to live on Earth, make our home here, eat what we want, have a good time, we should keep peace. We should teach our young people to be guided by love. Where do our young ones go to learn that?"

After about thirty minutes of conversation, Sam stood up, gathering the flowers back into his hand. "Come on, I'll show you my hogan." We hiked to the top of the trail, then down the road for another mile or two until we came to his dirt driveway. "I built this house twenty-five years ago," he said as we walked through the narrow opening into the hand-built log structure. The building was circular, with holes in the sides to let in light. There was a fire ring in the center for cooking, some pots and pans around, and Navajo blankets covering a cot.

Inside, on the dirt floor, we sat awhile longer as he told me tales of life on a Navajo reservation. I asked, "If you could be remembered for something, what would it be?"

"I am a good man, a good Navajo, an honest man, a US citizen—that's what I want to be remembered for," he told me. So simple. So clear.

Before I left, I asked if I could take his picture. He nodded, his eyes on the hands folded in his lap.

"Sit in the doorway," I told him, knowing this was a portrait I'd be sending back to him and wanting it free from clutter. It was Sam Reed's simplicity, his sincerity that I hoped to capture.

Weeks later, when I developed the film, I printed Sam's picture and sent him a few 8 x 10s. I never heard back, but always hoped that he liked them, hoped that he found in that image a reflection of "a good man, a good Navajo, an honest man, a US citizen." It was his own essence I wanted to give back to Sam Reed, in gratitude for the time he took to share it with me.

Taking pictures of people is a lot like creating characters for a story. Short story-writer Eudora Welty explains the connection this way in *The Eye of the Story:*

> I learned quickly enough when to click the shutter, but what I was becoming aware of more slowly was a story-writer's truth: the thing to wait on, to reach there in time for, is the moment in which people reveal themselves. You have to be ready. In yourself, you have to know the moment when you see it. The human face and the human body are eloquent in themselves, and a snapshot is a moment's glimpse (as a story may be a long look, a growing contemplation) into what never stops moving, never ceases to express for itself something of our common feeling.

It's that common feeling I mine for in my search to find another's essence, so I can

---

A better and less ignorant photographer would certainly have come up with better pictures, but not these pictures; for he hardly could have been as well positioned as I was, moving through the scene openly and yet invisibly because I was part of it, born into it.

EUDORA WELTY

record faithfully the greatness of the inner. Sam Reed and I lived opposite lives on opposite sides of the country. We had nothing concrete in common, and yet there was something inside him that was right here inside me, resonating with every sentence he uttered. What we shared was a matter of spirit, not body. And what I hoped to capture on a small strip of film was a sense of his greatness of spirit, his serene quietness.

This portrait of Sam Reed is a culmination of generosity, of risk, of openness, of two strangers trusting each other with the stories of their lives. It tells of a journey together, a trip from the expansive canyon to the inner sanctuary of the hogan and the inner lives of both of us. We shared as much of ourselves as we could, ending our time of communion

Professionally, one may have to stand outside the experience one is recording, but privately I want to be more a part of it.

RENÉ BURRI

with a ritual of image-making. To me, Sam's photograph is what Julia Cameron says portraits should be, *the embodiment of a prayer.*

Reflections

1. Imagine that a well-known photographer has invited you to his/her studio to make a portrait of you. You are asked to choose the props, the clothing, the background, the kind of lighting that best expresses who you are. What does your ideal portrait image look like? Are you smiling or serious? What background and props will you select? What clothing will you wear to express who you are? Will the photo be in color or black and white? Why?

2. Imagine that you are going to take a portrait of a person whom you know and care about—perhaps a spouse or partner, child or parent. Spend some time with that person just observing him or her closely, and see what expressions or actions best convey the person's essence. Have a conversation with the person about what you noticed, sharing the essential characteristic you'd like to shoot for. Discuss how this characteristic might be expressed photographically, and then make a portrait that satisfies both of you.

3. Plan a portrait day for your closest friends. Create a makeshift studio by putting a chair or stool in front of a white wall or a fence or patio door covered with a white sheet. Arrange your shoot in the daytime when there is good light, and be sure to have your models sit in indirect light rather than in sunlight. Invite your guests to outfit themselves in a way that captures something essential about who they are and to bring whatever props they need to fill out the scene. Shoot several portraits of each person so

you'll have plenty of images to select from when they're developed.

4. Choose one of the portraits illustrating this chapter and spend a few minutes looking into it. Imagine that you have spent a few hours in conversation with this person and that your talk has revealed some intimate details about her or his life. Write a few paragraphs from this person's perspective that reveal this essential truth or insight.

Photography gives us a chance to say, in more than words alone, what we believe in, where we stand. It is a form of expression that reveals not only who we are, but how the world appears through our eyes. There is some risk to this, but more importantly, there is that possibility that our revelation will touch another, heal some brokenness, lead us back to our wholeness.

CHAPTER 6

Speaking Our Peace

Find something you like to do. Learn to do it well, and do it in the service of the people.

KARLENE FAITH

L ong before I started photographing, I was moved by images that captured my attention and enhanced my awareness of the world at large. On many a rainy afternoon as a child, lost in the photo essays of *Life* and *National Geographic*, I entered the lives of people around the world, pondering the contrasts between my life and theirs.

In my teenage years, the violent images of the 60s sank into my heart, cutting short my innocence—the march on Selma, the assassinations of John F. Kennedy and Dr. Martin Luther King, the Vietnam War, and the Kent State shootings. Then, as now, I was impressionable—moved by what I saw, changed by what I experienced, led to action by what I believed.

Most of us, at some point, have a desire to make a difference in the world. We *want* our lives to matter, our words to be of use. Photographers and others whose medium is images want the images we put out into the world to speak eloquently about what

The photographer creates, evolves a better, more selective, more acute seeing eye by looking ever more sharply at what is going on in the world. The photograph may be presented as finely and artistically as you will, but to merit serious consideration, must be directly connected with the world we live in.

BERENICE ABBOTT

matters to us, to be the ambassadors of who we are, what we believe in, and what we stand for.

The roll call of photographers who lived by this principle is long and illustrious. Dorothea Lange left a successful studio photography business to work as a documentarian. Her images altered the public's consciousness about the plight of migrant workers. *Life* magazine photographer W. Eugene Smith understood the power of a well-structured picture story and created compelling photo essays on issues he felt strongly about, such as the industrial pollution at Minamata, Japan. Documentarian Walker Evans was committed to making photographs of tenant farmers that would inform and inspire people to action. Lewis Hine, in his crusade against child labor, created images that did what dry statistics and lengthy speeches never could. Photojournalist and humanist Robert Capa despised war and photographed five of them in an attempt to record its horror and monstrous stupidity, believing that "the truth is the best picture, the best propaganda."

Having seen the work of these great image-makers and activists and reading about the national response and social reforms their pictures generated, I understood the power that photographs could have on a level beyond the personal. I saw that images could help shape a national consciousness, creating an awareness that could lead to enlightenment, action, change.

Buoyed with this knowledge and faith, in the mid-80s, during the massive global buildup of nuclear weapons, I embarked on a peace pilgrimage around the world. Armed with two hundred rolls of film and a slideshow about the American peace movement, I set out to use my photographs *in the service of the people,* to share with as many folks as I could

Photography was conceived as a mirror of the universal elements and emotions of the everydayness of life . . . a mirror of the essential oneness of mankind.

EDWARD STEICHEN

A photo becomes not only an interpretation of a given place, not only an image to be appreciated for its own challenging beauty, not only a journalistic report of a given moment in time, but also an evocative release, a symbol—even at times a trigger to a stream of consciousness.

JOHN RUSKIN

images of an active commitment to peacemaking, harmony, and a safe home for all the world's children.

To create a culture that reflects a reverence for life, we need stories and symbols that heal and guide, that help us remember we are part of a whole. It's hard, in a society bent on power and profit, to remember what life is really for. Harder still to connect with one another when most things serve to keep us separate. But stories help. Pictures help. And

We receive the light, then we impart it. Thus we repair the world.

KABBALAH

Where there is no vision, the people perish.

PROVERBS 29:18

every contact with a lover of life brings us one step closer to loving our own. My journey was a search for those images and stories, an attempt to discover and reveal our oneness around the globe.

In Japan, I was invited to speak to a group of A-bomb survivors at the Nagasaki Association for the Promotion of Peace and to present my slideshow, *Focus on Peace*. Before my presentation, the program called for us to watch the premiere of a Japanese film that included recently released American military footage of the Nagasaki bombing.

I sat in the back of the room with Mr. Matsunaga, director of the organization, who served as my translator. The lights dimmed, and the film began with a slow pan of the Nagasaki Peace Park. Paper cranes and colorful flowers filled the frame. Then a jump cut took us to the cockpit of an American warplane on August 9, 1945.

We watched the bomb drop. Watched the deadly cloud devour the city. And then from the ground we watched what followed. Mr. Matsunaga, his calm voice silenced, collapsed into tears by my side. The survivors in front of us sat still as sculptures. Frozen in time, they stared ahead, some gasping as they saw images of themselves on the screen, stumbling through the rubble of charred corpses. Dazed and burned, survivors were calling for families they would never find. Quiet sobs filled the room as we witnessed the rerun of a nuclear holocaust.

When it was over, no one moved. No one turned on a light. We sat there in the dark amidst sobs and tears. When the lights came on, and I was introduced, I stood before them and started to cry. It was only at their urging that I could carry on.

I began to speak slowly about the slides we were going to see, with Mr. Matsunaga at my side translating. Then the lights went out again, the music started, and images of millions of people working for peace began to dissolve into each other. There were no words spoken in the slideshow, just the pictures and voices from the International Children's Choir singing "Let There Be Peace on Earth." The images of colorful, festive, life-affirming demonstrations had more power that day than any I remember. Symbols of a solemn commitment to peace washed over and comforted us. They delivered us, if only momentarily, from the fear that a nuclear holocaust might happen again, for how could these millions marching and chanting and praying for world peace *not* make a difference?

After the slideshow, the survivors came to the microphone one by one to speak of the profound impact the peace photographs had had on them: "I did not know so many people cared about what happened to us." "We thought we were all alone in our struggle." "Seeing that so many Americans care about peace encourages my efforts." "How can we fail if there are so many of us?"

I had been so immersed in the peace movement during those years that, until that day, it had not occurred to me that others around the world weren't even aware that there *was* an American peace movement doggedly resisting the production and proliferation of nuclear weapons. Finding out made a *difference* to these Japanese people, seeing those pictures, witnessing others in solidarity with them who were working as hard as they were for the same cause.

We will take photography in a life-moving direction when we photograph what we know and feel, when we image our own lives, when we publish the images that are ours. Seeing ourselves doing things we never imagined possible, we will begin to do them.

RUTH MOUNTAINGROVE

Art does not in fact prove anything. What it does is record one of those brief times, such as we each have and then forget, when we are allowed to understand that the Creation is whole.

ROBERT ADAMS

Those eighty images, one after another, blended with that music, had an impact, told a story that bolstered their courage, honored their experience. What had happened to them *did* matter after all, and these photographs were evidence of how much. Nothing in the world could heal their physical wounds, their irradiated organs, their burned and disfigured faces and limbs, but a healing did occur in their spirits that day, passed on through these portraits of comrades in action.

We can and do inspire each other in this life. If a photograph does nothing more than inspire one person to feel that somehow his life mattered, her pain served a purpose, then that one photograph must not go unseen. We can never know the reach of our work,

never know when we share a photograph how and why it might make a difference, never know how our small image might help clarify the whole global picture.

But what we do know, from our own experience and the experience of history, is that photographs can change the course of things, turn one's head, alter one's thoughts, enlighten one's darkness. To shoot with that awareness, to know our images, made of light, can contribute light—that is the true joy of photography.

When the eyes see what they have never seen before, the heart feels what it has never felt.

GRACIÁN

Reflections

1. Sort through your body of work, and see if any underlying themes surface. What things do you tend to focus on when you photograph? What do your images say about what's going on in the world these days? About what's going on in you? Could a stranger look at your work and discover something about who you are, what you care about?

I shall light a candle of understanding in thine heart, which shall not be put out.

II ESDRAS 14:25

2. What issues are being discussed in your local community? What images could you make that would reveal your opinion about these issues? If you were to make a poster defending your ideas about any of these concerns, what image and words would it contain?

3. Reflect on the photographs that have moved you in the course of your life. What images come to mind? What elements made them so powerful? Did any photograph or series of photos lead you to action of some sort? Which ones? Why? Do you know if your photos ever led to another's action?

4. If you were to have a photo essay published in *Life* magazine and the entire project would be funded so you could go anywhere and shoot anything you wanted, what would be the subject of your story?

We heal ourselves in the act of photographing by being fully present to the moment at hand. When we stand on the edge of that which is, we are released from the yoke of what has been, detached from the fear of what might be. There is only the moment, the light, the matter of our vision. All is peace in the eternal now.

CHAPTER 7

Mindful Seeing, Mindful Being

To make images is a way of ordering one's world, of exploring and understanding one's relationship to existence. . . . The images we make are often ahead of our understanding, but to say "yes" to a subject is also to have recognized, however dimly, a part of oneself; to live with that image, to accept its significance is perhaps to grow in understanding.

JOHN BLAKEMORE

When Dorothea Lange gave up her successful San Francisco portrait business to become a documentary photographer and voice for the disadvantaged, she was saying "yes" to a subject in which she recognized her own story. Lange knew suffering firsthand. Childhood polio had left her with a permanent limp. Her father abandoned the family when she was twelve, and her mother was so preoccupied that Dorothea spend much of her youth wandering the streets of New York's Bowery, learning to become invisible for safety's sake. Her adult life was no easier. Her marriage failed, her activities were circumscribed by debilitating illnesses, and she struggled to balance her gifts as a photographer with responsibility to her children.

In the 1930s, Lange became a photographer for the Farm Security Administration. Her difficult past fueled her empathy with her subjects, migrant workers set adrift by the

If you follow your bliss you put yourself on a kind of track that has been there all the while, waiting for you, and the life that you ought to be living is the one you are living. When you can see that, you begin to meet people who are in your field of bliss, and they open the doors to you. I say follow your bliss and don't be afraid and doors will open where you didn't know they were going to be.

JOSEPH CAMPBELL

I remember what has happened in my life through moments that I remember visually.

DOROTHEA LANGE

Great Depression. She attributed her visual skill to "some kind of memory the blood carries."

Through her lens she told the stories of these anonymous, voiceless, unrepresented Americans. Her images transformed their experiences into "everyone's experience" and articulated the nation's woundedness with penetrating vision and compassion. They caught the country's attention, altered its self-perception, and catalyzed significant social changes. It was Lange's photographs, in fact, that moved John Steinbeck to write *The Grapes of Wrath*.

In her later years, looking back over her accomplishments and struggles, Lange said in an interview: "I've been weary all my life, and I've always had to make a great effort to do the things that I really wanted to do, combating not having quite enough to do it with. . . . You do, really, what you must do. You can't deny what you must do, no matter what it costs."

Sick and fatigued as she was during much of her career, Dorothea Lange was driven by an "inner compulsion" that she identified as the vital ingredient in her work. Mindful of being the medium through which others could tell their stories, she was guided more by instinct than by plan. This instinct led Lange to retrace twenty miles on a rainy highway to search out, in a tent on a muddy field, the woman who would become the subject of her most famous photograph, "Migrant Mother."

Many of us can identify with this "inner compulsion." We have had the experience of following our instincts, never sure where or to whom they might lead us. We *know* that voice, that craving to dance to the inner beat, express our passions, create something new from the stuff of our lives. We know the rapture of being lost in the moment, the risk of going all out for a cause we believe in, and the willingness to sacrifice security for the sake of the work.

Artists tread frequently on this ragged edge. Many of us live week to week or month to month, never sure if the ends will meet. Few of us have retirement plans or the other trappings of financial security, but we wouldn't trade our freedom for any number of IRAs. We are driven by a belief in the value of our work, inspired by those artists who have gone before, who have contributed to the cultural landscape with little support or recognition.

I am inspired particularly in this regard by Laura Gilpin. In the 1930s, she began to photograph the Navajos, though her documentation was not of interest to government officials. For over thirty years, she worked with no support. Her grant requests were repeatedly turned down, and she had no prospects of publication. Nevertheless, she and her companion, Betsy Foster, traveled hundreds of miles through rough terrain with heavy equipment to record the last vestiges of a vanishing culture. Gilpin supported her passion with commercial work—portraits, Christmas cards, a photo essay on Georgia O'Keeffe for *House Beautiful.*

Gilpin's images are rich in intimacy, revealing the deep relationships she forged with the Navajos over many years. She was mindful about the whole process, never paying

One looks, looks long, and the world comes in.

JOSEPH CAMPBELL

people to model as did many of her contemporaries, but earning her way into their lives and hearts, returning year after year to the same families, building trust, building friendships.

Laura Gilpin was seventy-seven years old and on crutches when her book *The Enduring Navaho* was finally published. At the age of eighty-one, she received a grant from the School of American Research for a major study of the land and people of Canyon de Chelly in Arizona.

In *Why People Photograph*, essayist/photographer Robert Adams writes: "Some art is meant, I think, to help us as we rest, as we get ready to go out again. Laura Gilpin's pictures are of this kind. One opens books of them in anticipation of renewal."

One is equally renewed by Dorothea Lange's potent images of migrants. Both photographers immersed themselves fully in the experience and extended sincere empathy to the people they photographed. Their photography was a labor of love, a vehicle to heal their own woundedness, to communicate their own openness. Both just went out into the suffering world with eyes wide open, mindful and present, heartful and engaged.

As Lange put it, photographing instinctively in this way is "a very good way to work . . . to open yourself as wide as you can, which in itself is a difficult thing to do, just to be yourself like a piece of unexposed, sensitized material."

When one goes off to photograph, setting aside everything for this excursion of seeing, the rest of one's life is temporarily on hold. There is nothing to reckon with but the moment at hand, and within that moment, the only questions that cross the threshold of consciousness are whether the light is good, the background right.

When I am in the forest hunting for the image, nothing exists but the forest and me. Thoughts of past or future never enter my mind, nor am I haunted by concerns of how or why. With every ounce of energy focused on the looking, there is no attention left to feed annoying fears and doubts.

Every sense is working in the service of the eyes. I do not hear a concert when I am photographing it. I can only *see* that concert, as if my whole being had become an eye, all the atoms assembling themselves in support of the task, attentive to the nuance of each unfolding moment. And in that process, I am safe from life's terrors, protected by my focus and absolute attention on whatever is before me.

We are vulnerable to fear only when we leave the present. If I drift into the past, my regrets surge up, my memories of failing and forsaking. If I shift into the future, I meet with doubt and delusion, fear of what's to come, what I'm not capable of controlling. It's in the present moment that I belong. Only there do I feel my balance, find my oneness with all creatures, with all life, with the meadows and mountains.

We are yanked backward and forward by our earthly concerns, torn away from our center, from the calm of the moment we are part of and one with. Adrift, we collude unwittingly in our own imbalance, dwelling on old pain, both inflicted and absorbed. We wake up to our today's in fear of tomorrow, afraid we won't have enough, be enough, know enough to survive the unknown—while all the while, the known, the present, is right at hand.

Only through mindful awareness can we can escape this vortex; only through attentiveness can we keep ourselves focused and resist the seduction of past and future. In the process of photographing, we pull ourselves back to the present again, our eye on whatever whispers our name. We study this thing with reverent attention, until we sense its nature and our connection to it, until we see in it, however dimly, a part of ourselves. This is what heals us: this presence to the moment, this attentive looking, this discovery of our relationship with other living things.

Photographers have been looking since the first daguerreotype. We have journeyed to the ends of the Earth for what we might find, and we bring home what we can of life's grand offerings so that we can share the marvels our eyes have found. Photographer Ruth Bernhard said that "looking at everything as if for the first time reveals the commonplace to be utterly incredible, if only we can be alive to the newness of it." Alfred Stieglitz said that art is the "quintessence of wonder put into form." The most compelling photographs contain that wonder. The photos that grip us, call us back to themselves over and over—as do one's favorite poems or plays or concertos—those photos renew us, heal us, without a doubt.

It is good to remember the source of that healing, that it began in the soul of one who went looking, who brought back from the journey a mirror for us all.

Reflections

1. What attracts your attention when you are in nature? How does it make you feel? Do photographs of these things help you recapture that feeling? Try looking at some nature images or making some of your own, and see what happens.

2. Make an excursion to a place that brings you comfort. As you experience this peacefulness, see if you can discern what about it creates that sense of well-being. Make a photograph that contains as much of the essence of this place as you can. Enlarge the image, and hang it on your office wall.

3. Read one of Thich Nhat Hanh's books on mindfulness, such as *The Miracle of Mindfulness, Peace Is Every Step,* or *Being Peace.* Begin to practice mindfulness in your daily life, especially when you go out into the world with your camera.

If you do not see what is around you every day, what will you see when you go to Tangiers?

FREEMAN PATTERSON

The soul should always stand ajar, ready to welcome the ecstatic experience.

EMILY DICKINSON

Art seems to be a spark of the eternal coalesced with a distinct historic moment, driving artists to do something that witnesses their depth, that expresses their most personal and universal insights.

ALEX GREY

When we turn our lens on the human family, we are drawn more deeply into its richness and turmoil. Something of the other seeps into our lives, stakes its claim in the shafts of our conscience. Our questions deepen as we image life's tragedies, focus on its terrors. How do I shoot to reveal the light? What truth can I capture and carry to others?

CHAPTER 8

New Images for a New World

The ultimate aim of the quest must be neither release nor ecstasy for oneself, but the wisdom and power to serve others.

JOSEPH CAMPBELL

Each of us holds in our memory images that have affected us, changed our way of thinking, moved us to laughter, to tears, to action. Some of us are who we are today, doing what we are doing, because a photograph moved us in that direction. Images of world wars, famine, epidemics, and ecological disasters have raised consciousness and led to worldwide movements for peace, social justice, health care, environmentalism.

The root meaning of the word *document* is *docere,* "to teach." Whether we are documenting the evolution of our families or the revolution of a third-world country, the images we make are teaching tools. People will look at a photograph we make and learn something from it. In a split-second glance, they will take in information that will affect them, alter their consciousness in some way that they may not be able to articulate. But the impact will be immediate, loaded with potential.

Those of us engaged in documentary work have the power and the privilege of

If the doors of perception were cleansed, everything would appear to man as it is, infinite.

WILLIAM BLAKE

Utter truth is essential and that is what stirs me when I look through the camera.

MARGARET BOURKE-WHITE

shedding light on the issues we address. What's powerful is the capacity of our photographs to help shape another's thinking on a subject. The privilege is that we have the freedom to express our own opinions and passions through our work, that we can draw attention to whatever aspect of the subject we choose.

Our seeing is colored by our sensibility, our images powered by our emotion, by the intensity of our attention and the precision of our focus. No two photographers will reveal the same truth about a subject, for every subject contains multiple truths, profound complexities. Scientists have discovered that identical experiments have varying results depending on the consciousness of the observer. Likewise, photographic documents of the same event yield different results depending on the consciousness of the photographer.

A photographer opposed to nuclear energy, assigned to the task of documenting the local nuclear power plant, might come back with images of dead birds on the roof, stockpiles of dangerous waste products, employees suffering from a variety of health maladies, children in the neighborhood who have come down with leukemia. A photographer in favor of nuclear energy might document the restoration of natural waterways, families boating on a lake developed and maintained by the energy company, rooms full of computers and high-tech equipment ensuring the safety of all operations.

No matter how well trained we are to be neutral observers, it is difficult to separate our seeing from our feeling. I was once in a classroom where a young photojournalist shared what it was like for her to photograph an antiabortion rally. Pro-choice herself, she

Two qualities essential for a great photographer—insatiable curiosity about the world, about people and about life, and a precise sense of form.

BRASSAÏ

was upset by what she saw and struggled with the challenge of seeing it and recording it objectively. She referred to it as the worst photographic experience of her life. After she spoke, a young man took the floor and said that his worst experience was having to photograph a pro-choice rally, that being opposed to abortion, he struggled with the same concerns. Both knew that they could reflect in their images disdain or support, that the matter of their focus, their stance, their choice of angle, content, and composition, all contributed to images that ridiculed or dignified the event.

While these two photographers could not choose the subject they were photographing, they had a great deal of freedom in *how* they would photograph the event, as we all do whether we choose our subjects or are assigned to them. That's the creative challenge of the work, the question that we wrestle with as we determine what it is we want to convey through our images.

And although we may come to the task with a certain plan, a certain confidence about our point of view, it often happens that, along the way, something else is revealed; some new thing rises, coming to light on the surface of our film.

Years ago, while photographing for a Catholic newspaper, I was working on a photo essay about a rural shelter. A Catholic priest had converted a former TB sanitarium into a refuge for over a hundred homeless men caught in the snare of drugs and alcohol. My

When artists give form to revelation, their art can advance, deepen and potentially transform the consciousness of their community.

ALEX GREY

Significant images render insights beyond speech, beyond the kind of meaning speech defines.

JOSEPH CAMPBELL

personal quest was revealing through images the bondedness and community that these men were creating. Having experienced life in a religious community, I was eager to compare my experiences to this brotherhood of men, to see how they built bridges to each other, shared their burdens, passed along their wisdom as they grew in sobriety and self-awareness. I had volunteered at the shelter on weekends when the place had first opened, though twenty years had passed since that time and my return to the shelter as a photojournalist.

On the first day, I arrived with my camera round my neck, but with no intention to shoot till I had spoken to the men. Having cleared the way with the priest in charge, I set about making myself known to the men I would soon ask to reveal themselves to me. I walked into a cafeteria crowded with men awaiting their lunch and looked around for a face that seemed welcoming and friendly. Within moments I was greeted by Bill, a cheery old-timer who'd been a resident since the place opened.

He invited me to the table, asking who I'd come to photograph. I told him and the others at the table that I was there to do a picture story and to capture what I could of the community they were building. I went from table to table to introduce myself so that everyone would know who I was and what I was up to, meeting most often with grumpy responses or none at all.

I gravitated back to Bill, asking him about weekly activities, good times to be there, and sharing a little bit more of myself. Having received a colder reception than I expected from most of the men, I knew it would take some time to establish the kind of rapport I'd hoped for. When lunch was over, I followed a group into the card room and watched their afternoon rituals unfold—rituals that were repeated over and over, day after day, for the weeks that I spent gathering images. These four men in a card game; that one doodling on a sheet of paper in the corner; this one alone with his coffee and Camels; that one alone with a jigsaw puzzle; and most of the others alone in their rooms, having vanished immediately after the meal.

The artist enriches the soul of humanity. The artist delights people with a thousand unsuspected shades of feeling. The artist reveals spiritual riches until then unknown, and gives people new reasons for loving life, new inner lights to guide them.

RODIN

Although my original intent was to document "community," to portray in pictures fellowship in action, the more time I spent with this group of men, the more I realized my own illusions. I had come there to find joy, intimacy, a lightness of being, but these didn't exist, at least not in the way I saw them in my mind. For a while, I kept trying. I shot tight images of men together, waiting for something that looked like closeness, some hint of bonding. Hovering at the card table, I watched intently for the eruption of laughter, the hearty wholesome slap on the back, the sparkle in the eyes when contact is made.

Not finding what I was looking for in these gatherings, I meandered down hallways, past closed doors and the sounds of sleep, wondering what it felt like to live without intimacy, wondering if the closed doors concealed men who really wanted to keep others out or who just didn't know how to ask them in. Aside from meals three times a day, which were often consumed in relative silence, these men, loners for the most part, rarely ventured out into communal space. I eventually made friends with a few of them, sitting in

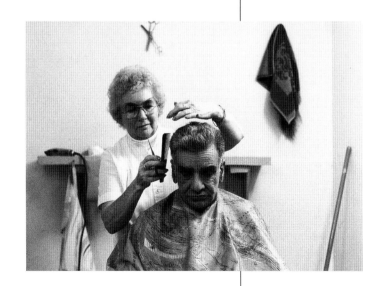

their rooms for hours at a time, listening to their stories of broken dreams, lives gone awry.

I felt, for the first time, an inauthentic quality in my shooting. I was lying about what I saw, cropping images to portray a sense of closeness, when isolation was the prevailing condition.

Finally, as a matter of integrity, I abandoned my desire to depict the kind of community I wanted the men in the shelter to have. As a result, I was free to make images of what I found—a group of men living private lives in a communal setting. In the end, what I recorded was more intimate, a story not about interaction but about individuals. In the process of shifting focus from the whole to its parts, I was gifted with the openness of each man I sat with, listened to, and recorded on film. Rather than telling the story of previously homeless men now harbored in a safe shelter, my eyes were opened to stories of abuse, of the agony of living with shattered hopes, the damage sustained by the human heart when intimacy disintegrates into isolation. It was *that* story I had come there to learn and to disclose, not some rose-colored portrayal of the brotherhood of man.

When we aim our cameras with integrity at the human condition, essential truths are revealed. Many photographers come to the task, as I did to the shelter, with unlimited passion and limited knowledge, projecting their own inner pictures onto the film before it's exposed. They know in advance what they want to say and search for evidence that supports their beliefs. And while it is crucial that we photographers come with our passion, it is wise to leave our "knowing" at the gate before we enter—wise to come as pioneers

seeing for the first time new frontiers, so that the story we tell will be purely its own, not a projection of our inner world, a reflection of desire or sincere determination.

When we set out to document something, we are tasked with revealing the essence, the true spirit of it, as we see it and feel it in our bones; for the more truth a photo contains, the more potential it has to touch the heart. As powerful images have inspired and informed us in the course of our lives, so might our images awaken others, ignite a passion, lead to an action that will save a life, a forest, a species.

These are dangerous times on earth—times of despair and disillusion, of mean-spirited greed and intolerance for "the other," times of reckless violence against nature, against each other, against our own overworked, overstressed selves. These are times when we, as imagemakers, can be of use.

Every time we load a roll of film into our cameras, we can choose to contribute something

My photographs are never straight reportage, never merely objective. In them all, I have expressed myself, nothing else.

ANDRÉ KERTÉSZ

valuable to the global family album or add to the stockpile of meaningless imagery. If we accept that photographs—our own included—have the power to lift us up, to change the world, what then shall we focus on, what stories shall we tell? What is it we care about, want to learn about? What do we know that we can pass on to others? What is missing that we might add?

This is our time to make things happen, our chance to throw ourselves into our passions, to make something of the gifts we have, to contribute to the healing of this fragile Earth and of those beautiful beings who cross our path.

Reflections

1. If you could create a picture story on a subject that would enlighten people and inspire them to a particular action, what subject would you choose? What action would you hope to inspire?

2. If you were called upon to document the homeless in your community, how would you go about doing this?

3. You are invited to speak to a college class of aspiring photojournalists. You will have fifteen minutes for the presentation. What will you talk about? What images will you share? What do you hope to convey?

The human face is the universal language. The same expressions are readable, understandable, all over the world. Its shades of meaning, its explosions of emotion and passion, all concentrate on just this part of the human anatomy, where a single twinge of just a few muscles runs the gamut of the person's potential. The key to understanding this language is having an educated heart. . . . The secret places of the heart are the real mainsprings of one's action.

DOROTHEA LANGE

What photographers are looking for is the life force, the heartbeat of what we encounter. While we cannot know in advance what shape this force will take, we recognize it instantly when we are in its presence. A gesture, a shape, a throw of light or depth of shadow moves us into another realm, ignites a memory or a vision of a deeper truth.

CHAPTER 9

Life Seeking Life

To see and know a place is a contemplative act. It means emptying our minds and letting what is there in all its multiplicity and endless variety come in.

GRETEL ERLICH

The whole world changes for me when I walk through it with my camera. On days when I walk for the sake of walking, with no camera in hand, my mind is besieged with random thoughts, breaking like waves on the shore of my being. I am pushed and pulled by the surge of them, like a strand of kelp below the sea, always moving in the ebb and flow.

On days when I walk for the sake of seeing, the act of looking consumes my consciousness. The mind quiets down, giving way to the eyes, and the world enters through the silent portals. What thoughts occur in that timeless movement seem not to come from outside myself, but to surface from a place deep within, rising from a soul in search of expression.

It is the soul, then, that seems to lead me forward, nudging me along as I forage for images that might reveal her. It is the metaphor I am after, that which points to something

For me, the creation of a photograph is experienced as a heightened emotional response, most akin to poetry and music, each image the culmination of a compelling impulse I cannot deny. Whether working with a human figure or a still life, I am deeply aware of my spiritual connection with it.

RUTH BERNHARD

What we are looking for is Who is looking.

ST. FRANCIS OF ASSISI

else, giving voice to an essence larger than language. My vision expands as I scan for signs of the Divine in the world. Is it there in the bend of the shallow river? There in the veins of the red maple leaf? There in the shimmering reflection of water, the rusty gate on the mountain path, the eyes of the woman huddling in that corner?

I'm drawn ever closer to the world I live in, drawn into its pulse, its beating heart, drawn into its pain and heart-wrenching passions. I sometimes cry at what I witness—rarely in sadness, most times in joy—stumbling into images that soothe me like a lullaby, reminding me of the smallness and hugeness of my life.

One Saturday afternoon when I was taking photographs on Fire Island, I was meandering along the wooden boardwalk and heard a strange clippety-clop sound behind me. Imagining it was someone in high heels, I never bothered to look back. The sound got louder and louder, as if the person were trying to catch up to me. When I finally turned around to see who was following me, I was stunned to see a whitetail fawn at my heels, looking up at me as if we belonged together. I held out my hand, and she nuzzled her wet little nose into my palm and followed me lovingly back into the woods. I had been looking intently for signs of life, and here was the wildest life of all, hot on my trail.

Another time in a redwood forest in Northern California, I passed by a small spray of wild irises in the early hours of dawn. They were tiny, purple-rimmed buds, folded in upon themselves and barely noticeable in the dimly lit

grove. I paid them hardly any notice, caught up as I was in the vastness of the redwoods, looking up, looking out for the bigger signs of life. After trudging through the woods for a few hours, I backtracked on the trail and sat down to rest on a burned-out stump. I had just caught my breath when a shaft of light streaming down from above cut a radiant path

I always photographed what the moment told me.

ANDRÉ KERTÉSZ

through the dense greenery. And there were those irises, full-fledged flowers, purple petals everywhere, leaning toward me as if they had something to say about life itself. Tears sprang to my eyes, and I finished off my film on my knees before them.

When Saul Bellow accepted the Nobel Prize for Literature in 1976, he spoke of "an immense painful longing for a broader, more flexible, fuller, more coherent, more comprehensive account of what we human beings are, who we are and what this life is for." The feeling Bellow described is soul longing, the longing that sparks creation. It is the *formless* yearning to be given *shape; feeling* wanting to be given *form*. This longing is felt in the heart of every creator, and every creation is a response to its call.

Dorothea Lange wrote that "artists are controlled by the life that beats in them, like

the ocean beats in on the shore. They're almost pursued; there's something constantly acting upon them from the outside world that shapes their existence. But it isn't other artists' work, or other artists; it's what belongs to the artist as a solitary." What belongs to each of us as artists is that unique voice, that singular calling from our deepest caverns.

We cannot respond to that call if our ears are tuned to the noise of the world, or if we look outside ourselves for direction. The world is full of people who call themselves authorities, who say it must be done this way or that. They will tell you to specialize, to choose one kind of photography and stick with it, that you can't be good at more than one thing, so for God's sake don't try to write, too. They'll say it's impossible to publish a photo book, that there's no market for your work because everyone's using stock photos, that you won't be taken seriously if you don't shoot this kind of film with that kind of camera. They'll say photography has nothing to do with the spirit, that it's a technical thing, more craft than art.

If you're not careful, you'll start to believe them. You'll cave in and think it's about money and being published and achieving notoriety, when the real thing behind your work has nothing to do with any of these, not at its core. The real thing is that sweet joy you feel when you're in the midst of it. The real thing is how present you are to life when you're working, as attuned to light as a lion is to scent; a hawk to a movement in the meadow below. The real thing about photography is that it brings you home to yourself, connects you to those things that fulfill your deepest longings.

The divine soul within us longs to be expressed. It is embodied in our physical beings in order to be made manifest in the world *through* us, through our creations. Just as we yearn to be drawn up into the heart of God, so God yearns to be drawn out into the heart of the world. It is life seeking Life; Life seeking life. The power of our art is ignited when these forces collide, flesh and spirit, human and Divine.

When we come to photography fully alive, and in the act of photographing, connect

Something deeply hidden had to be behind things.

ALBERT EINSTEIN

with the life force of what is before us, our images contain some of that vitality. They are potent, full of energy, powerful enough to draw another in. When the god-force within and the god-force without collide and lead to the creation of something new, we have found our "decisive moment," a compelling moment full of wonder and grace.

Reflections

1. Sit quietly, and imagine that within you is a part of Divinity that wants to be expressed through your work. How would you go about manifesting the Divine in your work?

2. Go for a walk with the explicit purpose of photographing the life force within things. Let your eyes be drawn to whatever attracts them. Notice what things you notice, and see if you can tell why you notice them. What are the life forces that draw you?

3. In response to an inner compulsion, Dorothea Lange left behind a successful business to photograph on behalf of the poor. She believed that artists are pursued by something acting upon them from the outside world that shapes their existence. Does this feel consistent with your experience? When was the last time you acted on an inner compulsion? What keeps you from doing this? If you knew you were to die next year, what would you do differently today?

The photograph carries on one continuous surface the trace or imprint of all that vision captures in one glance.

ROSALIND KRAUSS

Every exposure is a discovery, both in the revelation of subject and the thoughts and emotions of the photographer himself. The ultimate achievement is reached when all the elements of craft, content, and intention are so perfectly balanced that the image is an entity in spirit and form.

ROBERT DOTY

Whenever I'm tempted to speak of God, the words of Lao Tzu come to mind: "He who knows does not speak. He who speaks does not know." I think that God, like love, is more aptly defined by what it isn't than by what it is. I think of Meister Eckhart, the Christian mystic, who says that the ultimate leave-taking is the leaving of God for God—the final letting go of the limited concept for an experience of the real thing.

When I was young, I prayed to be a martyr. I wanted to show God and everyone else that I loved Him enough to die for him. I wanted to go into battle for Him, be another Joan of Arc, a hero for God's sake.

Now all that's changed. I wouldn't think of dying for God, but am doing my best to live for God—with God, in God, with God in me. There are no more lines of separation, only strands of connectedness. My eyes find God everywhere, in every living thing, creature, person, in every act of kindness, act of nature, act of grace.

Everywhere I look, there God is, looking back, looking straight back.

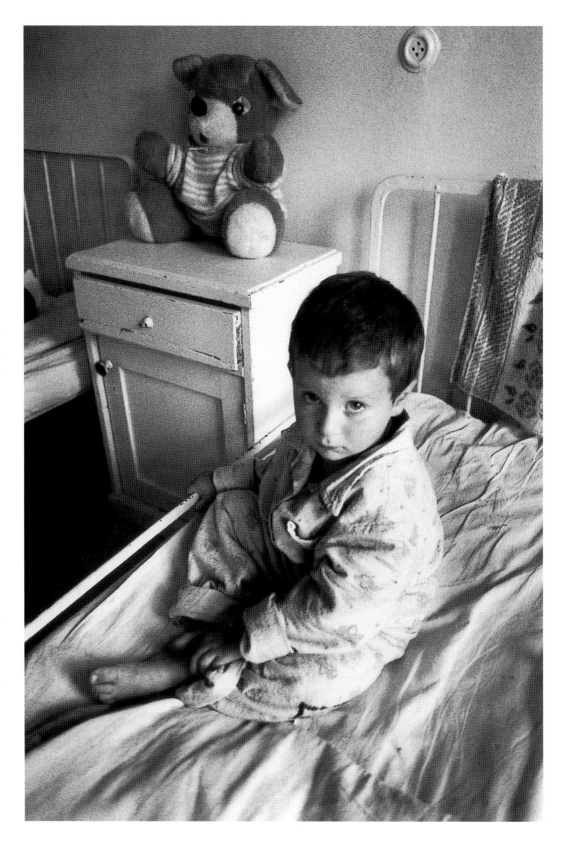

CHAPTER 10

God Is at Eye Level

I believe that God is in me as the sun is in the color and fragrance of a flower—the Light in my darkness, the Voice in my silence.

HELEN KELLER

I sometimes awaken from a dream hearing a faint whisper of words coming from a place that feels very far away. Dream telegrams, a friend calls them. Not long ago, I heard the voice again, this time whispering the words, "God is at eye level." I smiled myself awake, wishing I could talk back to this voice or visit the place where it was coming from.

The words lingered throughout the day, the weeks, and even now, when I'm out photographing, they are always there in the spaciousness of my mind. Through the woods, along the beach, in the streets of downtown, wherever I am with my camera around my neck, I hear that hushed voice—"God is at eye level," repeating over and over like a mantra.

At an early age, I learned that God was a particular Being who dwelled in a place far from wherever I stood. My perception of God has changed dramatically over the years. I am guided now not so much by teachings that have come down to me, but by learnings

The contemplation of things as they are, without error or confusion, without substitution or imposture, is in itself a nobler thing than a whole harvest of invention.

FRANCIS BACON
(posted on Dorothea Lange's darkroom door)

Self-realization is the greatest service we can render the world.

SRI RAMANA MAHARSHI

that have risen up from within—a shift that began thirty years ago when I was a young postulant taking my first theology class in a religious community.

The Jesuit priest stood in front of the room and asked each of us what we believed about God. One by one we recited our beliefs, recalling sentences from the Baltimore Catechism about who God was, why He made us, what He wanted from us. The priest challenged those beliefs one by one, tore them apart, belittled them as nothing more than memorized statements, versions of someone else's opinion.

He took a hammer to our naive image of God and shattered it. I started to cry, hating him, wondering how he could do this, how he could stand there and destroy God when we'd just given our whole lives over to God, left behind everything to *be with* God. It was a moment of devastating loss, incomprehensible sadness. I felt as if everything I believed in, everything on which I had based my life, were no longer true. The silence in the room was deafening; the void I felt, terrifying. We sat there, thirty of us, for what seemed an eternity, reckoning with the obliteration of God as we had known Him.

Finally the priest broke the silence. "You must come to know what is true about God from your own experience," he said. "Arrive at a faith that is deeper than your learning, one that is rooted in your ultimate concern and rises up from the nature of who you are." He said that we needed to let go of *beliefs* and conjure up a faith of commitment, one that rises up from within ourselves, from a deep awareness of our own godliness. The biblical paradox that says you must lose your life in order to find your life was beginning to make sense.

Self-realization is the actualization of our own divinity. It is a recognition of ourselves in all things and all things in ourselves, found through the simple contemplation of things as they are. The opposite of selfishness, it is a manifestation of ourselves as gift and mirror to others. The deeper one's self-awareness, the clearer the reflection one can offer.

Self-realization is an exploration into the complexities and contradictions of life, an attempt to plumb the opposites until we arrive finally at the oneness that contains them. It is a painstaking process of observation, an astute and relentless probing into reality, past our learned illusions of separateness into the profound experience of connectedness.

When we observe something deeply, we enter into it, become one with it. Something of its essence enters into us, and we are changed in the process. When we read a novel, see a play, listen to a story, we enter into its world, place ourselves in the scene and experience the drama and conflicts as if they were ours. We often come away from someone else's creation with a deeper understanding of our own story.

Italian poet and Nobel Prize winner Salvatore Quasimodo wrote that "poetry is the revelation of a feeling that the poet believes to be interior and personal but which the reader recognizes as his own." All things reveal us to ourselves. If we look deeply enough into an oak tree or mountain stream, into a photograph or other work of art, we will find

You do not have to imagine things. Reality gives you all you need.

ANDRÉ KERTÉSZ

ourselves there. And if we linger, listening intently, it will speak to us in a language divine, a language of light, symbol, metaphor.

In the process of observing, of being wholly attentive, we are liberated momentarily from our sense of separateness, rapt in a oneness with the subject of our gaze—a connection as real as lovers who have felt their spiritual beings merge in another dimension as their earthly bodies join together. We all crave this oneness, this holy and mystical union, and are willing to travel to the ends of the Earth to find it. Yet it is ours to experience in every moment, wherever we are. This oneness is the Tao, the ever-flowing reality—all in each of us and each in all. The accurate perception of our relationship to every living thing leads to awakening, to self-realization, to the experience and expression of God in the world through our artistic creations and through our compassion for one another.

Diarmuid O'Murchu, priest and social psychologist, writes in *Quantum Theology:* "Observation gives way to relationship, a complex mode of inter-acting, fluctuating between giving and receiving, until a sense of resonance emerges, whereby the individual parts lose their dualistic, independent identities, but rediscover a sense of the 'quantum self' in the interdependent relationship of the new whole, which might be anything from the marriage of two people to a newly felt bond with the universe itself."

Observation gives way to relationship, and relationship heals and sustains us. Whether with one other or with many, with children, with animals, with nature, it is our sense of relatedness that keeps us whole and balanced. In contemplating things as they are, we

The eye with which I see God is the same as that with which God sees me. My eye and the eye of God are one eye, one vision, one knowledge, and one love. My eye and the eye of God are one.

MEISTER ECKHART

experience the life force in living things, awaken to the consciousness throbbing in every being, every molecule and atom. On some profound and mysterious level, we fully understand our relation to the Whole. Only our thinking keeps us separate; only our beliefs keep us from finding the Divine in the substance of our daily lives.

In my quest for the Infinite, I have come to believe that God, Truth, Beauty, Love—all those concepts I associate with the Divine—are not things that are "found" at the end of the path, like the pot of gold at the end of the rainbow, but are rather what I experience on the journey as I travel through life—or perhaps, more explicitly, they are the journey itself.

God, to me, is the universe unfolding, the power and potential within all life, the Oak within our acorn selves. Not one bit separate, but fused with us like salt and the sea, ever-present in the faces, the scenes, the feelings that pass through our lives day to day.

When I pause long

Vision is freely given to those who ask to see.

COURSE IN MIRACLES

What cannot be seen with the eye, but that whereby the eye can see: know alone that to be Brahman, the Spirit; and not what people here adore.

KENA UPANISHAD, PART 1

Each artist is a facet of God's unfolding infinite vision, refracting the light of awareness in his or her own particular way.

ALEX GREY

enough to really look—as one must in the act of photographing—I am seized by this awareness, that everywhere I look, there God is. In the smooth gray bark of the eucalyptus, the immense bulk of the polar bear, the eyes of the hungry child, the angry customer, the tattooed teenager. I forget, when I'm not really looking, that something deep and beautiful is below the surface. But when I'm photographing, that is *all* I remember, all I seek to capture—that essence within things.

Photography heals because it reveals this essence. In the process of looking, finding, framing, shooting, all one's energies are focused purely. In the attempt to capture a piece of life in a fraction of a second, one waits mindfully, perfectly attentive, for the right alignment of shape and light, tone and texture, color and contrast. One waits for the cloud to come or go, for the child to forget there is anyone looking, for the fawn to rise up from its cozy bed of green. In these moments of waiting, a oneness occurs between the seer and the seen, and they become, knowingly or not, cocreators of an image that will endure beyond the present, have an effect, a healing power of their own.

As I think back on the inner voices that informed my looking before I knew I was seeking God at eye level, I'm conscious of a variety of them. When I first started photographing, the voice spoke a simple, "Don't forget this." I'd photograph people, places, events that had meaning and joy I didn't want to lose sight of. Photographing meant I could keep an image to savor later, reflect on, find myself in when I was lost.

Eventually, as I improved in the craft, another voice came along, whispering, "Share this." Then my looking was informed by a desire to pass along what I was seeing that another might miss. I photographed beautiful landscapes and flowers, put them into a slide

All of us living beings belong together,
inasmuch as we are all in reality sides
or aspects of one single being, which
may perhaps in Western terminology
be called God, while in the Upanishads
its name is Brahman.

ERWIN SCHRÖDINGER

show with music, and for the first time ventured out, sharing my images with the hope that they would lift up others as they'd lifted me.

In time, that voice gave way to another that said, "Your images can make a difference in the world—let them." As an activist for peace, I photographed disarmament rallies around the nation and traveled the world showing these images in an effort to reflect a consciousness of compassion and peace.

And as I traveled, among Buddhist, Hindu, Muslim, Communist, Arab, Israeli, Catholic, Protestant people—all of whom housed, fed, and nourished me in profound ways—the voice behind my looking changed to "You are one with each of these," and my photography grew in intimacy, in power, in conviction, colored forever by this new awareness of union, of nonseparateness, of family.

Though I can't know for certain if it's the same with all photographers, my guess is that all of our looking is informed by a deeper voice, a compelling passion that takes us to the edge from which we look and directs our gaze toward that which we seek.

Each of us listens to a different voice within, but if we are true to the voice that speaks in our hearts, the images we make will heal our wounds, mend our brokenness. If we think clearly and carefully about the power of our images, and in our looking, see past the barriers, the walls that have been constructed between one person and another, we may one day stumble upon the Divine we've been trying all along to find.

Reflections

1. Imagine that you are asked to create photographs representing the Divine. What might you include? What would you *not* include? Why?

2. Are there some people in your life you consider more "spiritual" than others? What are the qualities that contribute to this impression? How might you reveal this quality photographically?

3. Do you have a mantra or voice in your head that guides you as you shoot or paint or sketch or write? What is the primary motivation behind your image-making? Why?

In reality the main purpose of life is to raise everything that is profane to the level of the holy.

MARTIN BUBER

Nothing is a work of art which does not exhibit an infinite, either directly, or at least by reflection.

FRIEDRICH SCHELLING

God created humankind so that humankind might cultivate the earthly and create the heavenly.

HILDEGARDE OF BINGEN

It is not God who will save us, it is we who will save God—by battling, by creating, and by transmuting matter into spirit.

NIKOS KAZANTZAKIS

Many of us venture out into nature looking for signs of life with our cameras. We're moved by something and we shoot, unaware that there's more to the image than meets the eye, that it contains, perhaps, an answer to a question, a clue for our life's journey.

What if, on a walk through an oak grove, we followed our instincts and let our inner voice lead us to the oak that was calling to us? What if it were true that this oak had information for us, knew our concerns, held our solutions in its bark and branches, was waiting for us to sit down and listen to it? Would we go to that tree, give it our attention, listen in every way we knew how until we received its gifts for us? Would we suspend our disbelief in order to hear the answers we've been looking for?

Life is so hectic today it seems a ridiculous idea to spend any of our precious hours in search of a tree that has a message for us, but nature does hold some keys to our well-being and demands nothing in return but some time and attention. Whether we're in the desert, at the ocean, in a forest, there's an abundance of life there that mirrors our own, offers a perfect metaphor for our own changes and challenges. If we look deeply enough, we will find those symbols that are waiting for us, whispering our names into the breeze—perhaps in the trunk of a burned-out redwood, in the half-faded footprint on a desert dune. There are messages for us out there, words from the wild calling us home.

CHAPTER 11

The Thin Curved Line

The Desert, proclaiming itself, speaks gently. . . . If you and the Desert have found each other, surely you will feel the drawing of your soul toward the eternal calm—the brooding peace that is there in the gray country.

IDAH MEACHAM STROBRIDGE

A creative act is a process of conjuring up something visible from the invisible, of transforming a thought or experience into a form that can be perceived or encountered by another. Creativity is a universal human urge. We each yearn to express our experiences in such a way that others can know them vividly and sense their significance. Art emerges out of this urgency to share our inner lives, our visions and voices, fears and passions, and every work of art reveals something intimate about the artist.

Making art—being able to say what one sees that is whole—is an enormous relief, as if one had been held dumb by an impediment of speech and then abruptly cured, enabling one to say, and thus understand better, what it is that is most important.

ROBERT ADAMS

When I look into a mirror, I see my face, my body, the form of my being. When I look into my images, it is my soul that I find reflected, parts of myself that cannot be revealed in language. I could tell you about myself in puffed-up words, exaggerating my abilities, emphasizing my strengths, leaving out my flaws and failings, and you would walk away with a certain notion about who I am. If, instead, I handed you a box of my photographs and said, "This is the essence of who I am," your understanding of me would be truer, undistorted by language and interpretation. My photographs are a direct line to my inner world. They are the shortest distance between my soul and yours.

Even more important, my photographs are a direct line between my soul and me. As much as an image speaks of the thing seen, it speaks also of the person who photographs it. In *Photography of Natural Things*, Freeman Patterson writes that "the finest images—the images that stir our souls—combine documentation of natural things with a sense of what they mean to us." My take on a desert dune or a redwood forest is not only different from any other photographer's but reflects where I am emotionally and spiritually on the day when I'm shooting. If I am feeling fearful in the face of an oncoming storm, my image will contain a sense of that. If I am standing on a mountain top, awed by the grandeur, my awe will be reflected in the photograph I make. I listen for what my subject is saying to me, and once I know that, I can make a photograph that expresses both what it is and who I am as I see it.

Minor White said that the goal of the serious photographer is "to get from the tangible to the intangible, to render the image in such a way that it becomes a metaphor for something else—usually the photographer's state of mind." In his introduction to *Imogen Cunningham*, he wrote: "She likes to photograph anything that can be exposed to light, I remembered her saying. Only then did I realize that it was her own light—whether she admitted it or even knew it."

Griselda Pollock, in an article on women and media, extends this same sense of self-revelation to all creative work. "Art and the artist become reflexive," she wrote, "mystically

---

In my life, as in my work, I am motivated by a great yearning for balance and harmony beyond the realm of human experience, reaching for the essence of oneness with the universe.

RUTH BERNHARD

For me, the great event is when my awareness has risen to the point of perception, a brief but intense moment. I crave this feeling because of its greater clarity.

RALPH GIBSON

bound into an unbreakable circuit that produces the artist as the subject of the artwork

and the artwork as the means of contemplative access to that subject's 'transcendent' and

creative subjectivity."

I'm not a very technical person and for me cameras are just tools to do a job. The real camera is me. Without that little black box I couldn't transfer my feelings into images, but for all that it is still a tool. . . . Only the other night I went across the field and quietly took pictures of a pond over there that was half dried up. It was nine o'clock and there was hardly any light at all. I can't remember feeling happier in a long time. It was like a cleansing of my soul.

DON MCCULLIN

For those of us bent on self-discovery and the revelation of our own inward journeys, I can think of few better tools than a camera and film. For in that process of looking out to reveal our inner selves, we are on the edge of both, on that thin curved line between yin and yang, blending the known with the greater unknown.

It's not always clear to me when I make an image what use it will be to me later on. But when my eyes land on something, and I feel a chill in my bones, some kind of recognition, some sense of affinity with what I am looking at, I do whatever I have to do to get that photograph. It doesn't matter if I have to stop the car and get out in the middle of a downpour, climb up a mountain, wade into the chilly waters. It matters only that I honor my instincts, for the images that result are like clues to a treasure hunt, symbols that I can return to later when I am lost on the path, having forgotten who I am.

I'm assaulted daily by a barrage of media images that do not feed me. They drain me, insult me, discourage me, bewilder me. I return to my own photographs for balance. I am stilled and comforted, steadied and supported by images that called me in the past and still speak to me today.

When I see the photo of Buddha propped up on a box in the passenger seat of my old Honda, seat belted and ready for the ride, I'm both humored and consoled that I am wisely accompanied on my journey. When I see the footprints of my nephew Chad on the windblown dunes of the California desert, I taste again the fearless abandon of childhood, remembering that life is meant for adventure.

What I try to evoke in my photographs is the dynamic of the landscape, its spiritual and physical energy, its livingness, its essential mystery.

JOHN BLAKEMORE

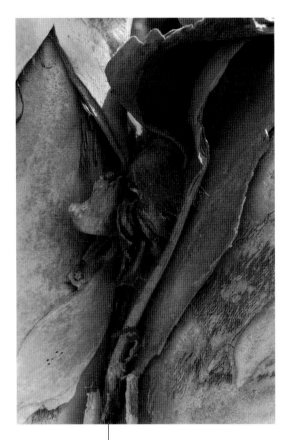

When I look at the velvety gray bark of the melaleuca tree or the smooth red rind of the manzanita, I'm stunned into reverence at the gifts of nature. And every image of sea and mountain reminds me of the suppleness and resilience of my own spirit and of the collective spirit of all human-kind.

When I see the toddler held in the safety of a warm tidepool as she peers out into the powerful Pacific, or the young surfer heading out bravely in search of waves that will scare and delight him, I'm grateful to my mother for taking me to the ocean's edge, holding my hand when I felt fear, and teaching me to step right out into it and through it, so I'd know how to do it when she wasn't at my side.

I'm comforted by the sight of vines climbing along rusty barbed-wire fences, invading fortresses long abandoned, cascading down walls of old mansions in ruins, because it reminds me that life will win out in the end. Human constructs and concepts will come and go, corrode and deteriorate, but the real life force, the spirit that surges through every living thing, is indomitable, unyielding, a metaphor for any of us caught in a struggle against negative forces.

I'm sure that people who glance at the photos on my wall, on my altar and desk, have no idea that they are seeing my Bible, my life's journal, my sourcebook of inspiration and comfort. They will see the earth, the sky, people, and places and never know that every

For the rest of my life, I want to reflect on what light is.

ALBERT EINSTEIN

image is a treasure chest of gold, that words of faith and sustenance and guidance are written all over each photo in bold, bright invisible ink.

When I go out with my camera into the desert, the forest, to the ocean's edge, and my eyes find solace in the sandy shadows, the soft bark of redwood, the ruffled edges of crashing waves, I make images that say to the dunes, the trees, "Here you are, and here I am in the presence of you." It is a mating, of sorts, a love song, two lovers caught in embrace.

And it is enough for me if no eyes but mine ever see the image that results from that encounter. For what I am looking for is what the place I am standing in *means* to me, knowing that if I see that image again, framed and hanging on my wall, that same meaning will return. Seeing it again will add to my dimension, expand my being with a single glance. No other viewer is needed, for no one could know anyway what they are seeing—what I found out about my own soul at that precise moment when I squeezed the shutter.

Reflections

1. Imagine that you have the chance to communicate something important about who you are to someone of great significance, but you can do this only through your photographs. If you had to select twenty images that would say what you wanted to say about who you are, what images would you use?

2. Look at the photographs in your home, and see what stories they contain. What do you feel or think of when you pass by them? How do they serve you?

3. Find a nature photograph in a book or calendar. Imagine that this image has a message for you encoded in its essence, that it has something valuable to say about your life and your future. Sit with this image quietly until that information comes through. What did you learn?

4. Invite a photographer friend to come over and bring a photo that has some personal significance. Select a photo of your own that has meaning for you. Agree to sit quietly for ten minutes with each other's photos, and see what feelings/ideas come to mind. Share your impressions about each other's photos first, and then take turns talking about your own.

For the most part, I have stopped reading newspapers and watching the local news. I ration my intake of global news. I am careful what radio stations I tune into and am quick to surf to another channel when the TV fare turns foul or mean.

I have learned what nourishes me and what doesn't, what is good to take in and better to leave out. But it still seeps in, the wails, the sirens, the horrible sound bites—ethnic cleansing, high-school murders, religious wars, domestic violence, corporate greed, child abuse, hate crimes, extinction of wildlife, and the list goes on.

It seems sometimes irresponsible, frivolous to write about spiritual concerns when the world around me is caving in, but I think, in the long run, it is spirit that will save us—the spirit that rises up in the rush of creation, a whoosh of pure energy, lighting our way through the dark unknown.

The answers to our crises will not come from outside, not from blaming, but will surface from within as we quiet our lives, call upon our wisdom, give voice to our souls in all the ways we can. Our world is hungry for creations that feed and sustain it—hungry for images, for music, for films and novels and poems and plays that wrestle with the issues and questions of the day, unfold their complexities, enliven our passions, and reawaken our drowsy imaginations.

It is from the Spirit that such works usher forth, and to the Spirit, then, that we must journey, each of us as a creator, bound for the Light.

CHAPTER 12

The Healing Nature of Creativity

There's something I would like to understand. And I don't think anyone can explain it. . . . There's your life. You begin it, feeling that it's something so precious and rare, so beautiful that it's like a sacred treasure. Now it's over, and it doesn't make any difference to anyone, and it isn't just that they are indifferent, it's just that they don't know, they don't know what it means, that treasure of mine, and there's something about it that they should understand. I don't understand it myself, but there's something that should be understood by all of us. Only what is it? What?

AYN RAND

It's not easy these days, making time for our creative work. Voices call us from everywhere demanding our attention, our energy. And many of us, somewhere along the line, got the message that making art is self-indulgent, so we relegate it to the bottom of our list. It becomes the thing we get to when the laundry is done, the bills are paid, the groceries are bought and put away, the lawn is mowed, the e-mail is answered.

We get so caught up in the flurry of our lives that we forget the essential thing about art—that the act of creating is a healing gesture, as sacred as prayer, as essential to the spirit as food is to the body. Our creative work reveals us to ourselves, allows us to transform our

What is to give light must endure burning.

VIKTOR FRANKL

By touching our deepest center, great art transmits the condition of the soul and awakens the healing power of spirit.

ALEX GREY

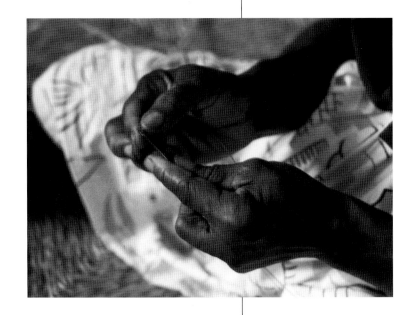

experience and imagination into forms that sing back to us in a language of symbol who we are, what we are becoming, what we have loved and feared. This is the alchemy of creation: that as I attempt to transmute a feeling or thought into an artistic form that can be experienced by another, I myself am added to, changed in the process.

As we center ourselves in the act of creating, attune to our inner voice, a shift occurs in our consciousness, allowing for the birth of something new. Our attention is no longer on time and demands and errands. It is caught up in the extraordinary metamorphosis of one thing into another. What begins as cocoon emerges a butterfly. What once was sorrow may now be a song.

Igor Stravinsky wrote of this shift in his *Memoir and Commentaries*: "My knowledge is activity. I discover it as I work, and know it while I am discovering it, but only in a very different way before and after. I do not try to 'think' in advance—I can only start to work and hope to leap a little in my spirit."

My own creative process unfolds in much the same way. It is not until I have actually started the work that any "inspiration" appears. I must begin first, and *then* the lift comes, the thrill of discovering something new as it reveals itself in the process of creating.

And just as I am changed by the art that passes through me in the process of becoming, so am I changed by the creations of others. When the photographs you make cross my threshold, they show me who I am in another light. I find fragments of myself mirrored in the eyes of your subjects, my joys reflected in the curve of their smiles. In the shades of your gray, the density of your blacks, the brightness of your whites, I find my own yearnings, my tears, my cries of delight.

I cover my walls with photos that move me and help me remember the whole of which I am part. When I wake up in the morning, photographs by Thomas Mangelsen are the first thing I see. His huge white polar bears dancing in the snow remind me of my bear-ness, my need to hibernate, to romp through nature hunting for that which feeds me.

When I come into my office and see Margaret Bourke-White's photograph of Mahatma Gandhi, or her image of two beautiful elderly women sitting on a cabin porch, I feel in the company of the loving faithful, doing as they did before me whatever they could to bring love and harmony to the world. When I look at my poster of Imogen Cunningham with the words "Never Give Up" under her smiling, wrinkled face, I'm buoyed up for another day of giving my best to the cause.

Throughout my house are portraits of strong and powerful women—old women, dancing women, women together, women isolated and alone—each in her own way,

The camera is an instrument that teaches people how to see without a camera.

Dorothea Lange

reflecting me, reminding me why I do what I do. When I look at that Bavarian woman on a train heading to Dachau, lost in deep thought as she peers out the window, I'm right back there with her, caught in my own quandary about the Holocaust of yesterday and the ethnic cleansings of today. Her image keeps me focused on my task, clear about my quest to inspire compassion, break through intolerance—my own and others'—in whatever way I can.

And as my eyes land on the photo of women's hands lifted in a ritual of healing and celebration, I shift internally from dark to light, moving from the shadow of our inhumanity to others into the brighter reality of our power to heal.

I am moved, in some way, by every image I encounter, as I am moved by music, poetry, plays, and novels. My tender heart is healed every time I hear Jimmy Santiago Baca reading his poem "Cry" in Bill Moyers' *Language of Life*. My mind is stretched and soothed whenever I read a Doris Lessing novel or an Adrienne Rich poem. Every part of my being opens up like a blossoming iris when I hear Richard Wagner's *Pilgrim's Chorus,* Pierre Mascagni's *Easter Hymn*, or the Benedictine Monks of Santo Domingo singing Gregorian chant. I'm lifted to new levels when I hear Ladysmith Black Mambazo's African mbube sounds or Israel Kamakawiwo'ole's haunting Hawaiian chants.

I am healed by the creations of others every day, conscious of the obstacles that each artist faced in the process of birthing them, and aware that if they did it, so can I; and if I do it, so can you.

For it is the same with all of us—we have our fears, our doubts, our cultures that negate the work of the spirit. And yet we continue on, journeying inward to find what is there that seeks release and offers comfort. Over and over, we transmute one thing into another, turning tragedies and triumphs into powerful images, colorful landscapes, haunting portraits in shades of gray. We conjure these images in our private hours and offer them to the whole like food for the soul, a wrap against the chill.

The call to create is a calling like no other, a voice within that howls for expression,

Everything that surrounds you can give you something.

ANDRÉ KERTÉSZ

Significant images render insights beyond speech, beyond the kinds of meaning speech defines.

JOSEPH CAMPBELL

the shadow longing to merge with the light. It is an act of faith to respond to this voice, to give it our time; in return we are blessed with work that has light and life of its own. One photograph can spark a revolution, thaw a frozen heart, inspire another's masterpiece.

Art that emerges from our inward journeys is a tale-telling mirror that collapses time and expands dimension. Our creations contain the past and the future, the known and the unknown, the breath of spirit and flesh of the body politic. As we respond to the world we are part of, what we create adds to its essence, changes its shape, heals its wounds.

No matter what the medium, art reveals us to ourselves and raises the level of human consciousness. Art is a mirror not only to the soul of the artist, but to the whole of civilization that celebrates its creation.

Simone Weil once wrote: "The work of art which I do not make, none other will ever make it." We, as creators, hold in our bones the lessons of history, paths to the future, glimpses of a world yet to come. The lines that we draw are lifelines, lines that connect, lines that sketch the contours of the future we're facing.

It is up to us—those who have felt the tug of that inner voice—to create the world we want to be a part of, to utter the words we want to inspire us.

Reflections

1. Look at the photographs you have on your walls or mantels or altars. Take some time with each one to see what healing it offers you. How are you affected by those images?

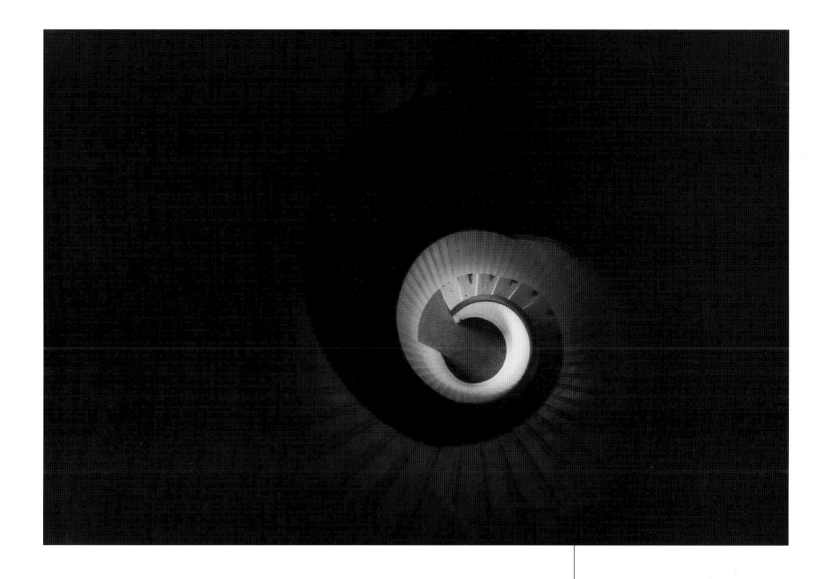

2. Look through your bookshelves and CD racks for your favorite works. What is it about particular music or books that lifts you up? What is the source of that power? How would your life be different without books or music or art?

3. Think of someone you know who is in need of healing. What kind of photograph might you make that would lift this person up by looking at it? Why not make that photograph and give it away as a gift?

A photograph should be a significant document, a penetrating statement that can be described in a very simple term—selectivity. . . . Pictures are wasted unless the motive power that impelled you to action is strong and stirring.

BERENICE ABBOTT

Of all the qualities that photography demands—an attentive eye, a focus on shape or compelling contrast, an attunement to color or range of grays— it gives back in kind an element of joy. There is sheer delight when, on the path looking for deeper things, we stumble onto images that lighten the spirit, lessen the load.

CHAPTER 13

Looking for the Joy of It

This natural world is only an image and material copy of a heavenly and spiritual pattern. . . . Thus the sage sees heaven reflected in Nature as in a mirror, and he pursues this Art, not for the sake of gold or silver, but for the love of the knowledge which it reveals.

SENDIVOGIUS (1750)

The Latin root of the word *amateur* is the verb *amare*, "to love." An amateur is someone who does something for the pleasure of it. For an amateur, the important thing is the experience, not the accomplishment.

Unfortunately, in our culture, the word has acquired negative connotations. It implies that someone does not measure up, that someone is not good enough to meet "professional" standards. This slur always annoys me and brings to mind the bumper sticker that reads "Question Authority." Who made up these "professional" standards anyway, I wonder, and why should I trust them?

Years ago I heard a definition of *amateur* that seemed much more to the point: The difference between an amateur and professional photographer is that the professional throws out more pictures!

When I first started shooting, my photo albums looked like a lot of other people's—

The act of making a photograph is less a question of what is being looked at than how.

MARGARET ATWOOD

Don't aim at success—the more you aim at it and make it a target, the more you are going to miss it. For success, like happiness, cannot be pursued; it must ensue . . . as the unintended side effect of one's personal dedication to a course greater than oneself.

VIKTOR FRANKL

blurry images, index fingers blocking half the frame, trees and lampposts jutting out of people's heads, tiny people lost in a vast landscape, faceless silhouettes against a gorgeous sunset. I had no control over anything. Amateur? Maybe so, but I had a great time taking pictures and treasured whatever I got.

Now that I understand more about light, my photo albums have a new look. When I come home with a new package of slides or prints, I sit down next to the wastebasket and eliminate mistakes immediately, before I form any attachment to them. Into the trash goes any image I do not like and any photo that I think would embarrass someone. For me, there is no need to hold onto photographs that do not shed light, bring joy, tell a story, evoke an emotion, reveal a person's inner beauty, capture an important moment in time, or reflect a piece of the world that touches my heart.

Those are the reasons I make photographs, and it is entirely up to me to throw them away if I am not satisfied with how well they meet my standards. I say this only because there seems to be some unwritten law in this culture that you must keep every photograph you ever made. Friends have looked at me horrified when they see me trash my mistakes, but some have started editing their own images, and their albums look a lot more "professional."

Each of us must answer for ourselves where the joy is in our work. If we get a kick out of recording our kids' birthday parties, our friends' weddings, our exotic vacations, because we want a record of those events, then it is fine to shoot away and stuff our albums with hundreds of images. The only rule is to have fun.

If our joy is in making images that look "professional," then we should have *that* awareness as we shoot—paying attention to the backgrounds, being clear about what we are focusing on, eliminating distractions from the scene, knowing what depth of field would accomplish our task, what shutter speed would work to stop the motion or create a blur.

One photography class is all it takes to understand the elements of control. And one simple, inexpensive manual camera is all it takes to make great photographs. It is your eye, your sensibility and awareness that matter in making a good image. For years, I shot only with a Pentax K-1000. All the photos in my first two books were taken with this camera and a few inexpensive lenses.

I've traveled around the world showing photographs, and invariably, particularly in this country, the first question people ask is what kind of camera I used to get those shots. Like it matters. You can drive across the country in a Ford or a Cadillac and the important thing is not the vehicle, it's *getting there*.

To get to the place you want to be with your photography, you do not need the best equipment; you need the best of *yourself*. You need to be aware of what turns you on, what feeds your hungers, what you love looking at, and why you love photographing it.

When people ask how I get such intimate shots of people, I tell them its because I

Art depends on there being affection in the creator's life, and an artist must find ways, like everyone else, to nourish it.

Robert Adams

Photographers undervalue the use of the wastebasket in their pursuit of fine photography.

RALPH STEINER

Each soul takes upon itself a particular task. . . . Whatever the task that your soul has agreed to, whatever its contract with the Universe, all of the experiences of your life serve to awaken within you the memory of that contract, and to prepare you to fulfill it.

GARY ZUKAV

Effort is the problem, not the solution.

DEEPAK CHOPRA

adore people. I love creating relationships, finding my commonness with strangers, building bridges from my world to theirs. That's the amateur in me, the one who loves intimacy, loves making images that reflect closeness and trust.

I don't have photographs of people I haven't spoken to or shared something of myself with. When I was preparing to travel around the world, I made a small album of my family to share with people. When I was with people whose language I couldn't speak, which was most of the time, I'd pull out my album, point to my mother's photo and say "Mama" or to my dad's saying "Papa." Everyone in the world understands those words. Showing those pictures to people opened up possibilities for some kind of relationship, even if most of the communication was in body language or baby words.

When I traveled around the United States photographing and interviewing people in small towns about their faith and values, I traveled with my book *Making Peace: One Woman's Journey Around the World* so they could see what I do, what kind of pictures I make and why. I couldn't ask people to disclose something important about themselves without my going first, without letting them know something about me. We don't end up with intimate relationships or intimate portraits without first giving something of ourselves away.

With landscapes, it's much easier and risk free. Out in nature, it is just us and the world, just the silence calming us down, flooding our eyes and senses with lush texture and colors. As we wander about, stalking the perfect shadow, the elegant form, we are lost in the moment, responding to the earth, oblivious to the human chaos we've left behind.

Figure out what it is you love about photography, and do that as often as you can. If you've wanted to experiment with a 4x5 camera, take a class and get on with it. If you want to shoot like Ansel Adams, read his book on the zone system. If you like nature, fill your walls with your own nature photos or make notecards from your photos and give them away. If you want to photograph wild animals, start a savings account for a photo safari in Kenya. If it's people you love, create an exhibition of interesting faces and characters in your neighborhood and show it at a local coffeehouse. Make a slideshow of twenty of your *best* vacation shots, invite a few friends over, and tell a two-minute story about each one. That'll take only forty minutes, and your viewers will love you!

There are countless ways to have fun with photography, no matter how serious we are about our photographs. Whether we do it for pay or simply for the love of it, we should not forget the joy it offers. From the moment our eyes light on a subject, through the time it takes to compose and focus, till the film is processed and the prints are in our hands,

The best way to make your dreams come true is to wake up.

KABIR

ready to be shared in whatever way we choose—through all these stages, there is great anticipation, the joy of wondering how to compose it, what it'll look like, if it'll be a winner worthy of a frame. We shift in the process from looking into, to looking forward, eager to see how the moment we captured looks on film. And what a delight if a shot stands out—perfect lighting, perfect background, perfect tone and expression!

When I was just starting out, an old-timer told me, "You're lucky if you get one winner out of a whole roll of film." I was so new to photography that everything in focus looked pretty good to me. Now, of course, an old-timer myself, I know exactly what he meant and agree completely. I jump for joy if I get one strong image out of thirty-six exposures, and if I don't, so what? I got my money's worth of fun just looking through that lens.

Reflections

1. Take a field trip to a local park with your family or a few friends. Make sure everyone has a camera, even if it's one of those inexpensive throwaways. Create an "assignment"—for instance, "take pictures of things that make you happy"—and give everyone a time limit to complete it. Then develop the prints, and compare the results.

2. Sit down with a few of your photo albums and a wastebasket. As you go through the pages, remove all the photos that are blurry, too dark, too light, not quite right for some reason or another. Take a deep breath; then throw them away.

Flow is the way people describe their state of mind when consciousness is harmoniously ordered, and they want to pursue whatever they are doing for its own sake.

MIHALY CSIKSZENTMIHALYI

The editors at **Life Magazine** once told *André Kertész that he was "talking too much with his photographs," a criticism that puzzled him, as it was his goal to create expressive photos. "You need expression to create a picture," he would say. "Everything that surrounds me provokes my feelings." Kertész created extraordinary images using the most ordinary scenes, often revealing his own emotions through the use of shadow, light, or imaginative juxtaposition.*

One need not travel to faraway places for dramatic images when the daily rituals of our lives are unfolding all around us, their poetry and meaning waiting to be recorded. If, through our images, we can reveal the heart of humanity, shine a light on what is precious and godly in ourselves and others, then let us find that in our midst and capture it in our lenses. Let us not wait for the heroic, conspicuous gestures, but rather look more carefully for those small, daily kindnesses, those rituals of bonding and sharing that show us as people revering life, revering each other. Our sensibilities are assaulted on a daily basis by a press consumed with portraying destruction. Heartbreaking photos of a world run amok wash over our days, invade our dreams. The shadow of humanity makes the news, while the light goes unnoticed, the good unrevealed.

May we, as image makers, shapers of the culture, set our sights on things we value, rituals we engage in that heal and serve. May our images honor the ordinary endeavors of common people, and may they make their way to the eyes of the weary—light to the dark, fire to the chill.

CHAPTER 14

Photographing the Rituals of Our Lives

I never had to go very far for subjects—they were always on my doorstep.

ANDRÉ KERTÉSZ

Most people, when asked what worldly possessions they would try to save if their house were on fire, mention photographs. "I could replace everything else," they say. "My pictures are my most precious possession. My whole life is in those photo albums."

Photographs provide evidence that our lives have meant something. They show our relationships with people, the places we've traveled, the events we've celebrated and honored. Of all the things that happen to us in the course of our lives, the most important get photographed, put into the shoeboxes and albums that we leave behind as legacies. Photos are our autobiography, a way of telling the tale of who we are.

I once visited a woman in Germany who had created a photo album for each of her four children. It was not a collection of haphazard snapshots edited together out of a huge stash in the closet, but a carefully conceived and

There is only one moment when a picture is there, and an instant later it is gone forever. My memory is full of those images that were lost.

MARGARET BOURKE-WHITE

laid out work of art. Each album was a beautifully bound leather book, and every photograph in it was perfectly composed, elegantly lit, dramatically designed, and placed on the page surrounded by lush amounts of white space.

This woman never referred to herself as a photographer, but these were some of the most touching portraits I had ever seen, taken on family vacations, summer trips to the mountains, weekend excursions in the Volkswagen van. She was making art of family rituals—an act that called for nothing more than attention and love.

In the course of our lives, we are all witnesses to events that honor the passages, the triumphs and tragedies of human existence. Whether these are moments of birth, death, communal gatherings, revolutions, rallies, or family reunions, they signify and symbolize our connection with each other, our commitment to something bigger than ourselves. These rituals keep us bonded, buoyant in the face of turbulence, bound together in spirit when our journeys move us apart.

When my father died suddenly and I flew home for the services, my camera was the only thing I thought to take. It was as if photography could help me get through my grief, help me channel my sorrow into something other than tears, give me something else to focus on besides my loss. When the family gathered, I photographed everything. In a way, it seemed an odd thing to be doing, recording all that sadness, but as I looked through my lens, it wasn't just sadness I saw. I saw intimacy; I saw reaching out and leaning into; I saw people arriving from faraway places to be there for each other, to speak about my dad and honor him in the best way they could.

The photographs are surprisingly beautiful and tender, showing people in all their seriousness, people in each other's arms, people off by themselves with their own thoughts about life and death. There are no big group shots, no lineups of happy people with cheesy smiles. The images are like a movie with no sound—and no self-consciousness. No one was putting effort into looking right. People were consumed with the moment, with their own private mourning, with comforting those of us most devastated by the loss.

In order to "give a meaning to the world," one has to feel involved in what he frames through the viewfinder.

HENRI CARTIER-BRESSON

My family now has an album of those days. It shows the tribe united, its powerful bonds evident in these images of compassion. The album is a reminder that out of each dying, something is resurrected; some new life rises up out of each one that returns to dust. It's a reminder that we are not alone, that people will come to us in our need, offer solace, be there when we cry out. Seeing those images and remembering these truths comforts me like nothing else.

When I think of all the rituals we engage in over the course of our lives, I'm amazed at how few of them get recorded. An exception, of course, is the wedding, which is documented religiously. Millions of dollars are spent annually in the service of this tradition, and no one ever questions it. We hand over a thousand or two to a photographer we don't even know, who spends most of the day trotting around trying to line up the right people at the right time for group shots. For a few hundred more, we can get the groom's face to

Photography has something to do with resurrection. . . . The survival of this image has depended on the luck of a picture made by a provincial photographer who, an indifferent mediator, himself long since dead, did not know that what he was making permanent was the truth—the truth to me.

ROLAND BARNES

It takes a lot of imagination to be a good photographer. You need less imagination to be a painter, because you can invent things. But in photography everything is so ordinary; it takes a lot of looking before you learn to see the ordinary.

DAVID BAILEY

show up in a bubble over the bride's head as she puts on her makeup before the ceremony or a composite of the couple in sexy soft-focus overlaid onto a champagne glass.

A whole industry is built up on all this glitz and glamour, but what of the other rituals we engage in? What images are we gathering of events, large and small, that mark the passages of our lives? How can we, as photographers, document the history of our families, our lives, our communities in a way that shows what matters to us, what forces bring us together?

Many of us belong to social, religious, and community organizations. We come together in these groups conscious that the whole is greater than the sum of the parts and that working collectively can heal not only our brokenness but the brokenness of the world. We plan events, take part in fund-raisers, organize conferences that help us identify and respond to hungers both internal and external. This common work is a ritual of bridging, of building community, of creating and celebrating affinity. This ritual is worthy of witness, of documentation, and we, as photographers, can expand the potential of the work by creating and sharing images of it.

It is an easy thing to produce a slide show of music, images, and words that portray the unfolding of a group's mission and values. Giving back to people a reflection of themselves in action, giving service, living out their faith or their commitments, is a tremendous gift. And it heals us to make these images, to place ourselves in the context of compassion

Intensified observations lead to exciting discoveries.

RUTH BERNHARD

and service, to bring to the table our gifts of visual discernment and delight. Like those who teach what they need to learn, we must photograph what we need to see.

Years ago, I went along to photograph my mother competing in the Senior Games. Her events were over by midmorning, and though I had planned to leave when she was finished competing, the atmosphere at the games was so magnetic, I couldn't tear myself away. There was more life, more vigor and joy and kinship there than I had witnessed in a long time.

I stood next to a woman photographing the pole vault event, watching eighty-something-year-old men hurl their lean bodies over a bar six feet high. Both of us had our cameras glued to our faces, and when she lowered hers to reload film, tears were streaming down her cheeks. "This is the most touching experience I've ever had," she told me. "The most beautiful thing I've ever photographed."

A seventy-one-year-old from Pennsylvania was warming up on the sidelines, bending, testing, and checking his pole. "When I read about the pole event, I realized there wasn't much competition, so I decided to take it up," he told me. "My kids were ready to beat me up when I came home with a pole one day, but it's been a great sport to compete in. I racewalk, too. Used to be I could win going backwards, but now there are so many competitors, I never win, but I keep on trying."

Another pole vaulter admitted he was jittery about the event. The week before, he had collided with someone while playing volleyball, and he still had a few stitches in his

forehead. He was so nervous about hitting the bar that, when his turn came, he soared over it like a gymnast, with several feet between his body and the bar. "I used to think I ought to give it up," he said, "until I watched a man with a wooden leg in the racewalking event. He struggled and struggled around that track, his face full of pain, his legs wobbling under the pressure. He was the last to come in, but everyone was cheering him on. When he crossed the finish line, the crowd roared like I'll never forget. Ever since then, I'm committed to these games."

As I walked around the infield, photographing competitors warming up and stretching, taping their javelins, checking their times, wrapping their ankles, I was caught off guard by the emotions that surfaced. There was something magical, something almost holy about being in the presence of five thousand elders who were risking all and reaching beyond the norm, passing their courage like a baton in a relay to anyone ready to take it.

In the way that the spirit is uplifted by music, transformed by art, calmed by prayer, it is also empowered by collective endeavor. It was that collective spirit, the enthusiasm and earnestness of these athletes, that touched me so deeply.

After watching the women's long jump for seventy- to seventy-five-year-olds, I walked up to the competitors who were congratulating each other. I meant to ask them

A saint's gift to us is a life, but an artist's is mainly a vision.

ROBERT ADAMS

I couldn't stay with the mountains, and I couldn't stay with the trees, and I couldn't stay with the rivers. But I can always stay with people because they are really different.

IMOGEN CUNNINGHAM

how it felt to be Senior Olympians, but when my lip started to quiver, I asked instead, "Why do these events make me cry?"

A jumper who had just won a silver medal said, "You're looking deep into the future here. Watching all of us do this lets you know that you will be able to do this, too, and your kids will be able to do this, and their kids. We're passing on a dream, a possibility, a hope for the future—isn't that worth a tear or two?"

Such ceremonies and rituals heal us in the beholding. A deep joy arises when we're witness to unity, focusing on community. For us to see and reveal our collective love for life, to make images of people stretching their limits, contributing what they have to the common good—this is the gift photography offers for the eyes and the soul.

If we peek into the photo albums of most American families to see what we generally find worthy of photographic attention, we might see birthday parties, religious holidays, and vacation getaways. But if we look beyond these, to those rituals and occasions that help us remember who we are and what we honor, more ideas for photography will come to mind.

It is time for us to bring into the world images of healing and harmony. Time for us to say we've had enough pictures of war horrors and Hollywood celebrities. Time to add our own visions to the archives of history, to tell our version of life as it unfolds before our eyes.

Reflections

1. Use your own family as the subject of a photo essay. Imagine that you are trying to share with a family from another culture what a week in the life of your family looks like. Document the rituals that you all engage in—your waking hours, the preparation for school and work, the meals you share, the evening hours, the activities you do for fun and relaxation.

2. Create a picture story called "One Square Block." Choose one block in your community, and walk around that block during different times of day just noticing what draws your eye. Notice how the light changes things, what shadows occur at different times, how dawn lights up one side or dusk another. Once you have noticed the drama of different light against different subjects, go out with your camera and photograph whatever is compelling. Consider enlarging and mounting your best images and hanging them in a bank or library or restaurant in your community.

3. Ask the oldest member of your family for permission to do a photo study of his or her daily life. Set aside a few days to be with that person, and create a character study that reveals all that you can about who this person is.

4. Volunteer your time as a photographer to a local organization that is serving the needy in your community. Offer to document their work and accompany members of the staff or volunteers on the job. Create a photo essay for the local newspaper or a national publication that tells the story of the group and its work. Use your gifts to contribute positive images of people helping people in a variety of ways.

I knew in a flash I wanted that, and found out a lot more afterward, editing it. You're trying for something, and if it's wrong you know it later on. But first you get it on the film, you garner it in. It's transcendent, you feel it. It's there, the ravished transcendent. . . . It's there and you can't unfeel it.

WALKER EVANS

Beauty will save the world.

FEODOR DOSTOYEVSKY

The photographs we make have a life of their own. And many have stories attached to them, stories that reveal us to another or others to themselves, stories that warm us like a sit by the fire. Sharing these stories can enhance our work, extend its reach, bring to light what else is hiding behind and around the image we see.

CHAPTER 15

Through the Lens and Beyond

As in a mirror, the responsive observer will discover not only the artist's reflection in his work, but his own image as well. In this way, we share our findings with each other, communicate and fill a deep human need.

RUTH BERNHARD

Having educated myself in the art of photography, I was not exposed to a great deal of critical thinking on the subject, which was OK with me, since it was critical *seeing* I was really interested in. After many years of immersing myself in the craft, attending hundreds of photographic exhibitions, reading every photography book and magazine I could get my hands on, I felt that I had a fairly good understanding of the photographic world. Even its unwritten laws, its unspoken protocols had seeped into my awareness, including certain expectations when it came to public exhibitions of one's work.

One such unwritten rule was that photographers should exhibit their pictures without supporting text. There seems to be a general consensus that accompanying text indicates a weakness in the work, as if words were needed to bolster images that were not muscular enough to stand on their own.

The basis of meaningful photography is then, for me, intensity of relationship, an obsessive fascination with the subject, with the attempt to see more deeply. To move from the visible to the invisible, from surface to process.

JOHN BLAKEMORE

A photographer's files are in a sense his autobiography.

DOROTHEA LANGE

One day I happened onto a traditional hula festival in Hawaii and was mesmerized by one dancer's elegance and power. Mapuana moved across the stage like an Earth Mother Warrior Goddess, chanting the story of her people's past. My eyes were glued to her every move.

Years later, this image of the hula dancer was printed as a notecard and made its way around the country. A woman who had received this card in the mail wrote me these words:

"Dear Jan, When I looked at this card I started to cry. I have always been fat and always hated my body, but when I saw that picture of Mapuana, I saw myself in her. I saw my beauty and my power, and for the first time in my life, I felt like I could love myself. I keep it on my altar now as a reminder of all the beauty that big can hold. Thank you for taking her picture and sharing it."

I used to ride past this farm on my way to work. Every summer, when the peas were ripe, these two women took their seats and started to shuck. Whenever I'd drive by, just the sight of them delighted me. They were always in the same place, always talking and giggling and shelling away, performing the same ritual year after year. They couldn't imagine why I wanted to photograph them, and they never once looked up as I circled around them, shooting away. We get lost in our rituals, and when we're in the midst of them, nothing else seems to matter. That's the healing thing about them.

Looking at this image, I'm transported right back there—I can smell the hay, hear the murmur of their voices, feel the same calm and joy that rose up in their presence.

Chairs, even empty chairs, have such a presence about them. I once passed by a circle of empty chairs in the Adirondacks and could have sworn I heard whispers and murmurs and giggles. Chairs embody the spirit of the people who sat there, holding in their realm an essence unseen.

I think in time we'll be able to see that essence; we will draw back the curtain between this world and that and enter into the fullness of vision, past duality into the One.

Being a newcomer to the profession, I accepted this policy and exhibited my work in what felt like a shroud of silence. Despite my desire to contextualize some photographs, to express what preceded or followed the captured moment, I hung them without captions on museum walls, deferring to what felt like sacred tradition.

Years later, while working in a picture-framing gallery, I watched people browsing the photos on the wall, unaware that I had taken them. Sometimes when they'd pause in front of a portrait, I'd let them know I was the photographer and could answer any questions they might have. They often asked where it was taken, and I would tell the story of why this person caught my eye, how it happened that the image was born, what unfolded in the course of the shooting.

As I told these stories, a bigger slice of history came to life. The image became a jumping-off point for a deeper conversation about what we stop to look at, what satisfies our visual hunger, what it is in the faces of strangers that calls us to them and leads to the intimacy of a photographic encounter. These details are the back story of the photograph. They are not essential to the art, but they can certainly enhance one's experience of it.

The same is true of a poem. A poem has its own magic whether we read it in private or hear the poet read it. But to hear the poet talk about the work, tell us what led up to it, what happened in the course of creating it, why or for whom it was written—these things expand the potential of the piece. They add a dimension, just as knowing about a composer's passions or madness or frailties enlarges our capacity to listen to and understand a symphony.

All photographs have a back story. While a photograph I make represents a fraction of a second in real time, it contains, in a sense, my entire history. When someone asks me

When I was growing up in a small village in upstate New York, I was the youngest kid on the block, still peddling my tricycle when everyone else had a two-wheeler. On Saturday mornings we would all start out, heading for the Little Red Bridge which was a mile away. Halfway there we'd come to the hill where the line would be drawn between them and me.

I could never make it to the top on my tricycle, and time and again, with tears splashing down my cheeks, I'd race back down the hill in search of my mom. On my lucky days, she'd swoop me up, dry my tears, pack up a picnic for the two of us, and off we'd go to the gazebo in the cemetery down the street.

This all comes back to me when I see a tricycle now, looming like an archetype in my mind—that eagerness to be bigger and to be one of the gang, the sorrow at being left behind, the solace I felt in my mother's arms. I photograph tricycles wherever I go for the comfort that they offer, the memories they stir.

Boats have a mysterious hold over me, symbols of the passage we are making from one state of being to the next. They can be a metaphor for so many things: serenity, connectedness, calm in the storm, humble living, opulence. I never see just a boat anymore. I see what it means to me, what it brings up on this day at this hour. Boats are like parables. We just need to listen and let them tell us their story.

how long it took to get this shot or that, I'm tempted to answer, "My whole life." Every moment led up to my being the kind of person who would take this photograph of that subject. Every portrait I make is a revelation of my longing for relationship and my ability to create it. Photography is a bridge from me to another, and when I describe the history of any portrait, I'm telling of the journey from my world to theirs.

A photograph does not exist merely as a thing in itself, but as a means to something else, a way to another place. When I look at the portraits on my wall, I travel beyond the faces into my memories of those people. When I pass by the image of the Greek widow winding her way down the narrow alley, I'm remembering how she laughed at the thought of me following her, shooting from behind. How she leaned on my arm and led me to her home, where she fed me tea and grapes and showed me every photo in her house.

The stories that we tell about our images are not about image making, but about the human qualities that surface in the process of being with another, of *seeing* that other through the lens and beyond. The healing aspect of photography is that it often leads us to these moments of togetherness, drawing us to those people whose spirit attracts us for some reason—and we come away with a picture of the kindness of people and the yearning that we all have to be truly seen by another.

Having come to trust my own authority, I no longer hesitate to include such stories when I exhibit my photographs, knowing that they add breadth and dimension to a visual that can very well stand on its own. While images convey their own poignant magic, which is beyond the scope of any language, the stories we tell about our pictures can extend their reach, bring to light new ways of bridging the distance from one person to another.

If exposure is essential, still more so is the reflection.

EUDORA WELTY

My challenge is to reach inside myself to catch the essence of a person—or what I feel is an essence. There cannot be one definitive picture. Human beings, gems that we are, have many facets.

ROLLIE MCKENNA

We think of photographs as the captured past. But some photographs are like DNA. In them you can read your whole future.

ANNE MICHAELS

Images exist not to be believed but to be interrogated.

ANDY GRUNDBERG

I was walking through a Beijing park at dawn and was startled to hear the sound of Chinese opera. Following the music, I came across a woman who was standing on the edge of a hill singing. I stood there quietly, rapt in attention, until she finished and looked my way. When I asked if I could take her picture, she smiled briefly, then went back to her music. I never got her name but have always thought of her as Beijing Morning Bird.

This photo was also printed as a notecard and made its way to a woman who was struggling to make peace with her own aging process. When she received the card and looked at this face, saw all those wrinkles, something shifted in her feeling about age. This is what she wrote about it:

"I have a new role model for this adventurous new country I'm now entering. She is a very old, wrinkled, rosy, beautiful woman standing in the morning light of a park in Beijing. . . . Now, she smiles at me every morning from my mantel. I love this woman. I like to think that, walking on the path ahead of me, she looks a lot like my future self."

This is the reach of our work, the potential of our images, the power of our stories. What we create adds to the world. What you see and speak of matters, has an energy, sheds light. Do not hesitate to share your creations. There may be someone who needs to see what you've seen, who is waiting to hear the story you haven't yet told.

A Balinese dancer once said, "There's someone out there who needs you. You must live your life so that person can find you." Good advice.

Reflections

1. Take one of your favorite photographs, and write the story that's behind it. Why did you take it? What did it mean to you? What else was going on at the time?

2. Join forces with another photographer or two, and produce a small exhibit of words and images on a theme. Hang your images in a local restaurant or coffeehouse. On a table near the images, put a journal in which people are invited to write their responses.

3. Find a few images from your childhood that include you and some members of your family. When you are with those family members again, bring out the snapshots and ask each one to tell the story of what was going on for them on the day the photo was taken.

4. If you have children, ask them to write a story about themselves based on a few of their early photographs. Put these words and images together into a book, make a cover with a title and their name as author, and present it to them as a present on some special occasion.

Explicit interpretation of photographs is determined mainly by the discourse that surrounds them.

CAROL SQUIERS

To take photographs is to hold one's breath when all faculties converge in the face of fleeting reality. It is at that moment that mastering an image becomes a great physical and intellectual joy.

HENRI CARTIER-BRESSON

To the extent that the photographer tries to make his work anything but what he is, he waters down whatever of value he has to give it.

RALPH STEINER

Mystics and sages have long held that Divinity is within us, of us, that all life is One Life, imbued with the same sacredness, worthy of our reverence and adoration. As we grow in this awareness, becoming more intimate with ourselves, with nature, with each other, more attuned to the spirit within, our capacity to see and feel and heal expands.

We see what is missing and offer that. We feel where there is pain, and place our hands upon it. We come to cherish life, to offer ourselves in service, in joy. And our work then becomes meaningful, useful, blissful.

If you wonder how to find passion in your life, look to see where you are needed, and go there joyfully, full of fire and loving-kindness. Focus your eye on every detail, every expression, every movement, and do not look away until you have seen the Divine. This is the vision, the awareness that will heal our wounds, repair our brokenness, and safeguard this world for those to come.

This, and nothing less.

CHAPTER 16

Photo Synthesis: Life from Light

I am sure—as sure as anyone can be of anything—that in the end there will be light, an all-pervading insight illuminating the immense structure of the cosmos, revealing the rightful place and purpose of man.

ANDREAS FEININGER

T hese are amazing and perplexing times we live in, full of wonder and contradiction. Creativity is rampant, as is violence and destruction. While scientific discoveries are enabling us to create and prolong life, technological advances are giving us the means to destroy it with increasing precision and magnitude. Though people around the world are linked through sophisticated communications technology, our cities are overflowing with lost souls, homeless and isolated. Some of us are struggling to find meaning in our lives, but even more are struggling simply to stay alive.

Henri Bergson, in *The Two Sources of Morality and Religion*, writes of humanity laboring under the weight of its own inventions. It is as if we have grown too far ahead of ourselves, added to the body but not the soul, so that the extension of our physical capabilities is out of proportion to the refinement of our spirit. "Now, in this excessively

Humanity groans half-crushed under the weight of the advances it has made. It does not know sufficiently that its future depends on itself. It is for it, above all, to make up its mind if it wishes to continue to live.

HENRI BERGSON

What is within is also without. What is without is also within. He who sees difference between what is within and what is without goes forevermore from death to death.

THE VEDAS

enlarged body," he writes, "the spirit remains what it was, too small now to fill it, too feeble to direct it. . . . Let us add that this increased body awaits a supplement of the soul and that the mechanism demands a mysticism."

To me, mysticism implies a heightened awareness of our oneness with all life, human and divine. Without this consciousness guiding us, grounding us, we abuse the technology we have so brilliantly conceived and constructed. Mysticism is demanded because we are poised on the perilous edge, at the brink where our choices will determine not what the future will bring, but whether there will *be* a future.

Teilhard de Chardin wrote that "humanity is being taken to the place where it will have to choose between suicide and adoration." The only light powerful enough to guide us as we make this choice is enlightenment, a supplement to the soul, the mysticism to which Bergson refers. If we do not come to terms with our own divinity and the divinity of others, our choice will be informed not by reverence and adoration but by illusion and self-interest.

Each of us is contributing daily to the creation of our common future, for better or worse, through our images, words, actions, and works. The more awareness we bring to the task, the more useful, the more compelling are our creations. The capacity to reach the highest states of awareness through contemplation, compassion, and grace is not limited to clerics, sages, saints. Any one of us can embark on that journey, find divinity in every detail, work at dissolving dualities and experiencing oneness in our own minds and lives.

As creators, photographers, visionaries, we are contributing images to the collective consciousness. The images we put out into the world inform those who see them. They carry weight. They add light, or not. They can expand the circle of human compassion, illustrate our relatedness, raise our global consciousness. And as our consciousness changes, so, too, do our relationships, our actions and interactions.

Once when I was producing an annual report for a nonprofit agency, I had to get photographs at the company's three worksites. Since I wasn't sure of the locations, I was provided with a driver, a young woman who worked as

a janitor at one of the sites. It was a blizzardy day, traffic was slow, and we spent about an hour together in the car driving around.

I didn't know anything about this young woman, so I started asking questions about her life, what she was interested in, what she liked about her job, if she had a family. Somehow, she ended up sharing a great deal about herself, about her father's alcoholism, her abuse as a child, her husband's violence, her fears for her kids, her determination to set out on her own and make a better life for herself and her children.

All I did was listen as the snow swirled and blew around us. After I had gotten my photographs, she dropped me off back where we started. But something big had happened

Our whole business in this life is to restore to health the eye of the heart whereby God can be seen.

St. Augustine

If the path before you is clear, you're probably on someone else's.

Joseph Campbell

between us, a bond was forged out of her telling and my listening, and from then on, whenever we saw each other, that bond was the first thing that came to mind. Our interactions were never the same after that talk. They had a new quality, an intimacy, an understanding, some kind of trust. We each could have asked anything of the other, it seemed, because we had gone such a distance together already.

Our relationships with people are vital and constantly changing. The more we give, the more we receive. The more we seek, the more we find. Finding God at eye level takes little more than attention, intention, and commitment. It requires that we give up our illusion of separateness and see ourselves in those refugees across the world, in those homeless men and women in the park down the street, in a young woman doing her best in a hard and scary life. It means giving up what we've learned about God being in charge and becoming healers ourselves, healing with our images, our words, our listening. It means staying faithful in the face of darkness, knowing that God is unfolding before us in every moment, in every story that someone shares.

Photographer Robert Adams asserted that art can help us make sense of all that is wonderful and all that is terrible about the world we inhabit. "Art," he writes, "is a discovery of harmony, a vision of disparities reconciled, of shape beneath confusion." Photographer and critic Tee Corinne speaks about art luring us beyond the confusion of opposites into a vision of the wholeness we seek: "The images we see, as a culture, help define and expand our dreams, our perceptions of what is possible. Pictures of who we are help us visualize who we can be." Alfred Stieglitz put it all more simply: "Art is the affirmation of life."

The photographs we make can be food for the soul, nourishing sustenance for the arduous and confusing journey we're on. We are all hungry for meaning, all on a quest to realize our worth, actualize our potential, manifest whatever is unique to us.

None of us is aiming for triteness, pursuing the shallow. It's greatness we're after—and not some hollow applause coming from somewhere beyond us, but the deep-down thrill of knowing we went all out, put our soul into the thing, created something that turned someone's head, sparked new growth. We want our fire to show, to flare up and light the piece of night that someone's shivering into. We want our work to be hot, to burn with reality and honesty, to ignite ideas and kindness and passion, to spread hope like wildfire through this darkness.

We're a culture in big trouble, making big mistakes, and everyone knows it. Just look at the ads, the meaningless sitcoms, the violence in every media format that exists. We need help, and it's the artists who must deliver it, because it's the soul that needs rescuing, buoying up, and that's where art goes. That's where it performs its magic, does it healing.

Creative work is not self-indulgent. It is not foolhardy. It is not pointless or trivial. It is crucial to our own healing and the healing of the planet. We each have a vision that no one else has, a way of seeing that is rooted in the particularity of our lives. I do not know what you know, cannot see what you see, unless you reveal that to me through your words, your images, your reflections. Your life is a

Whoever does not see God in every place does not see God in any place.
RABBI ELIMELECH

poem that the rest of us are waiting to hear, learn from, integrate into our own.

We photographers are poets in the language of symbols. We crystallize experience, reflect the essence of a moment, convey raw and honest emotion with contrast instead of cadence, composition instead of rhyme, light and shadow instead of words. "The creative process itself—with its beauty and elegance, but also its pain and destructibility—is our primary, tangible source for experiencing the divine energy," writes Diarmuid O'Murchu. This act of witnessing, recording the magnificent strivings and failings of humanity, this commitment to looking, to seeing into and through our daily lives—this is what centers us, grounds us in the Ground of Being, heals us and reminds us that we are not alone in our struggles and successes.

One might imagine upon seeing an imprint of five fingers through a frosty pane of glass that they were five separate circles, unattached. But a deeper truth arises at second sight. We are bound to each other and to this planet in ways impossible to speak of. Joseph Campbell wrote that "if we think of ourselves as coming out of the earth, rather than having been thrown here from somewhere else, you see that we are the earth, we are the consciousness of the earth. These are the eyes of the earth. And this is the voice of the

Those who have no compassion for themselves have none for others either.

RABBI MEIR

The real moment of success is not the moment apparent to the crowd.

GEORGE BERNARD SHAW

GOD IS AT EYE LEVEL

earth." We are not separate from, not above nor below. We are of the whole, part of the One. The same force that moves the planets, unfolds the petals of a rosebud, surges through a bolt of lighting, runs through us. Consciousness is embedded in all creation and awaits nothing but a fuller sense of awakening, a deeper awareness of the oneness of things.

When I look at your photographs, or you at mine, we catch a glimpse of that oneness. Everything around us is a mirror to who we are. If you tell me a parable, I learn a lesson for my life. If you read me a poem about dying, I feel in my bones every heartbreaking death I've witnessed. If I see a Monet or listen to Mozart, my spirit travels out to a more public place, to revel with others in the presence of such beauty. That is why a photo of a woman in Hawaii can help a woman in Nebraska break through some barrier to self-love, and why a portrait of one woman's wrinkled face can ease another's transition into aging. We are all hungry for the same nourishment, all vessels filled from one universal stream of human emotion.

It is art that transcends our illusions of difference, utters what we have long forgotten—that there is only one human nature and each of us is a single facet, constantly changing, reflecting each other's light and shadow. May the art that we create add fire to the world, light and wonder, healing and joy for ourselves and others.

Reflections

1. Give some thought to what the "sacred" is in your life and to the spiritual truths that guide you on your path. Make a photo excursion, and gather images that reflect this sense of sacredness and illustrate the essential oneness of all beings.

I must, before I die, find some way to say the essential thing that is in me, that I have never said yet—a thing that is not love or hate or pity or scorn, but the very breath of life, fierce and coming from far away, bringing into human life the vastness and fearful passionless force of non-human things.

BERTRAND RUSSELL

Some day, after we have mastered the winds, the waves, the tides and gravity, we shall harness the energies of love. Then, for the second time, man will have discovered fire.

TEILHARD DE CHARDIN

It is almost impossible for an individual alone to dissent from this culture. Alternative cultures and communities must be built up to support the dissenting consciousness.

ROSEMARY RADFORD REUTHER

Eventually I discovered for myself the utterly simple prescription for creativity: be intensely yourself. Don't try to be outstanding; don't try to be a success; don't try to do pictures for others to look at—just please yourself.

RALPH STEINER

Resources

SYRACUSE CULTURAL WORKERS (SCW) is an educational and cultural organization founded in 1982. Its mission is to create a culture that honors diversity and celebrates community, that inspires and nurtures justice, equality, and freedom. For a catalog, call (315) 474-1132; toll-free FAX (877) 265-5399; scw@syrculturalworkers.org; www.syrculturalworkers.org

INTERNATIONAL WOMEN'S WRITING GUILD (IWWG) is a network for the personal and professional empowerment of women through writing. Founded in 1976, with 3500 members around the globe, IWWG offers conferences and workshops, networking resources, a newsletter, and publishing connections to all women regardless of portfolio. (212) 737-7536; www.iwwg.com

CREATIVE EDUCATION FOUNDATION is a nonprofit organization committed to nurturing creativity, innovation, and problem solving in order to help individuals and organizations reach their creative potential. 1-800-447-2774; www.cef-cpsi.org

THE REAL WOMEN PROJECT is a collection of bronze sculptures and poems celebrating the diversity and beauty of women's bodies as they progress through the stages of life. The Real Women series is featured in The Changing Face of Women's Health, an exhibit that is touring the major science museums in the U.S. For information on exhibits or workshops, www.realwomenproject.com; (619) 683-7500

THE FOUNDATION FOR WOMEN is a nonprofit organization dedicated to nurturing, empowering and educating women in creating a better life for themselves and their families. 1-888-303-2622; www.foundationforwomen.org

More light!

GOETHE

(last words)

Recommended Readings

Adams, Robert. *Why People Photograph*. New York: Aperture Foundation, 1994.

Berger, John. *About Looking*. New York: Vintage International, 1991.

Bruce, Chris. *After Art: Rethinking 150 Years of Photography*. New York: Henry Gallery Association, 1995.

Capra, Fritjof. *The Tao of Physics*. Toronto: Bantam Books, 1984.

Cornell, Judith. *Drawing the Light from Within*. Wheaton, Ill.: Quest Books, 1997.

Davidov, Judith Fryer. *Women's Camera Work*. Durham: Duke University Press, 1998.

Eckhart, Meister. *Selected Writing*. Translated by Oliver Davies. London: Penguin Books, 1994.

Feininger, Andreas. *Roots of Art—Sketchbook of a Photographer*. New York: Viking Press, 1975.

Freind, David, ed. *More Reflections on the Meaning of Life*. Boston: Little, Brown, and Company, 1992.

Gendler, Ruth, ed. *Changing Light*. New York: HarperCollins Publishers, 1991.

Grey, Alex. *The Mission of Art*. Boston: Shambhala Publications, Inc., 1998.

Harvey, Andrew, and Anne Baring. *The Mystic Vision*. San Francisco: HarperSanFrancisco, 1995.

Harvey, Andrew, and Mark Matousek. *Dialogues with a Modern Mystic*. Wheaton, Ill.: Quest Books, 1994.

Heron, Liz, and Val Williams. *Illuminations—Women Writing on Photography from the 1850s to the Present*. Durham: Duke University Press, 1996.

Johnson, Robert A. *Inner Work*. New York: HarperCollins Publishers, 1986.

Kertész, André. *Kertész on Kertész: A Self Portrait*. New York: Abbeville Press, 1983.

Monk, Lorraine. *Photos That Changed the World*. New York: Doubleday, 1989.

Morris, Wright. *Photographs and Words*. San Francisco: Friends of Photography, 1982.

Mutén, Burleigh, ed. *Return of the Great Goddess*. New York: Stewart, Tabori and Chang,

O'Murchu, Diarmuid. *Quantum Theology*. New York: Crossroad Publishing, 1998.

Patterson, Freeman. *Photography of Natural Things*. New York: Van Nostrand Reinhold Ltd., 1982.

Steiner, Ralph. *A Point of View*. New York: Columbia University Press, 1978.

Zukav, Gary. *The Seat of the Soul*. New York: Simon and Schuster, 1989.

About the Author

Jan Phillips is a writer, speaker, and dynamic workshop presenter who has given seminars to over ten thousand people in twenty-three countries. She has appeared on radio and television, and her work has been published in the *New York Times, Ms. Magazine, Christian Science Monitor, National Catholic Reporter, Utne Reader*, and other international publications. As cofounder of Creativedge, she offers workshops that enhance creativity and communication in the workplace and facilitates transformational seminars for groups of individuals and organizations across the country.

Jan's most recent book, *Marry Your Muse: Making a Lasting Commitment to Your Creativity*, won the Publishers Marketing Association's Benjamin Franklin Award in 1998 as best self-help/psychology title and the Athena Award for Book as Mentor. She is also author of *Making Peace: One Woman's Journey Around the World*.

For information on Jan's workshops, call 1-888-820-4298, or visit her website, www.janphillips.com

QUEST BOOKS

are published by

The Theosophical Society in America,

Wheaton, Illinois 60189-0270,

a branch of a world fellowship,

a membership organization

dedicated to the promotion of the unity of

humanity and the encouragement of the study of

religion, philosophy, and science, to the end that

we may better understand ourselves and our place in

the universe. The Society stands for complete

freedom of individual search and belief.

For further information about its activities,

write, call 1-800-669-1571, e-mail olcott@theosophia.org,

or consult its Web page: http://www.theosophical.org

The Theosophical Publishing House

is aided by the generous support of

THE KERN FOUNDATION,

a trust established by Herbert A. Kern

and dedicated to Theosophical education.